BACK STREET NEW WORLDS

A Look at Immigrants in Britain

By the same author

WITH FORKS AND HOPE
(*An African Notebook*)

ON THE EDGE OF THE RIFT
(*Memories of Kenya*)

THE FLAME TREES OF THIKA
(*Memories of an African Childhood*)

A NEW EARTH
(*An Experiment in Colonialism*)

Novels

THE INCIDENT AT THE MERRY HIPPO

THE RED ROCK WILDERNESS

THE WALLED CITY

Back Street
New Worlds

A LOOK AT IMMIGRANTS IN BRITAIN

by Elspeth Huxley

WILLIAM MORROW AND COMPANY
NEW YORK

Published in Great Britain in 1964.

Published in the United States in 1965.

Printed in the United States of America.

Library of Congress Catalog Card Number 65–14952

Contents

JUN 1966

Introduction

Towards the end of 1963 the editor of *Punch* invited me to take a look at the various minorities who have settled in Britain, or are in process of so doing, from the Jews who came mainly in the 1880s to the Pakistanis who are arriving today. The outcome was a series called "Settlers in Britain," which appeared in *Punch* early in 1964.

The probing eyes of sociologists and other academics are being increasingly directed towards these immigrants, of whom over a million have arrived to stay since the end of World War II. Many studies have been made, or are in train, into the composition, behaviour, and needs of these various groups, from Caribbeans to Cypriots, Italians to Chinese. But so far no attempt seems to have been made to look at the subject as a whole and from a strictly nonacademic point of view—the angle of that mythical creature the man in the street.

Today that man (or woman), as he goes about the street, sees an ever increasing number of strange faces of all colours, casts of feature, ages, and kinds. He sees fellow citizens clad in unfamiliar clothing—women in baggy trousers, men in curls—and finds exotic foods he's never heard of displayed in the shops. Dusky men and women conduct and drive his buses, work beside him at the factory bench, and attend to him in hospital; children without a word of English sit next to his in school.

Suddenly a colour problem—something hitherto confined strictly to colonial situations and the United States—has cropped up on his doorstep; while he marches with his banner to protest against apartheid in South Africa, his neighbour may be turning away a coloured lodger and the value of his own property diminishing because a Negro has bought the house next door.

All this, of course, calls for careful study and the close analysis that sociologists can apply; it also raises various simple questions in the minds of ordinary folk. Who are all these immigrants, where have they come from and why? How many are there, will they continue to come, how can the British in their congested island pack them all in? Will they stay for good or go home? What about housing, overcrowding, hospitals, and schools? Are they being treated fairly, and what about us—are we being hypocritical, condemning race prejudice in others while displaying it ourselves? What about intermarriage? The housing racket? Employment? Health?

To begin to answer half these questions would take volumes and years. Certainly a handful of pieces, reprinted from a weekly magazine, can do no more than take a superficial look at some of the more obvious features of the scene. Perhaps, however, they may serve as an introduction to a situation of great interest and complexity. Some of the original *Punch* articles have been expanded, a section added about students, and a brief bibliography picks out a few of the many studies recently published. Others are on the way: notably one just started into race relations in Britain with the aid of a £70,000* grant from the Nuffield Foundation, under the auspices of the Institute of Race Relations and the direction of Mr. E. J. B. Rose.

Many busy people have been extremely generous with their time in helping me, and I am very grateful to all of them. More especially am I grateful to the staff of the Institute of Race Relations, under the direction of Mr. Philip Mason, C.B.E.; notably to Mrs. Sheila Patterson, editor of its monthly *News Letter*, who very kindly checked the manuscript—which involves her in absolutely no responsibility for any of the statements or opinions it contains—and to the Librarian, Miss Narinder Uberoi.

I should also like to thank especially Mr. Eric Butterworth, of the Institute of Adult Education and Extra-Mural Studies at the University of Leeds, who gave me so much help in Leeds and Bradford; Mr. Alan Gibbs and Mr. Geoffrey Ayre, who performed similar services in Birmingham; Miss D. M. Wood, O.B.E., of the Council of Social Service in Nottingham, and her opposite number in Bedford, Mrs. York; Miss Nadine Peppard, O.B.E., then of the London Council of Social Service; the Reverend David Mason of the Notting Hill Methodist Church, who enabled me to catch a glimpse of Caribbean life in Paddington and North Kensington; Dr. Ernest Krausz and Mr. Louis Saipe, who passed on a little of their knowledge about Jews in Leeds; Mr. Ben Parkin, M.P., who instructed me in housing rackets; Mr. Hamza Alavi and Mr. T. Ahmed, on whose intimate knowledge of Pakistani life in London I was enabled to draw; Mr. T. Kawwa whose studies of Cypriot schoolchildren were so valuable a source; and to the many education officers, headmasters, and headmistresses; the health inspectors and visitors; the managers

* About $196,000, the current exchange rate being $2.80 for one pound.

and welfare officers of firms employing immigrant labour; the officials of such bodies as the Royal College of Nursing, the National Coal Board, London Transport, the Anglo-Egyptian Aid Society, the Ministry of Health, the Departments of Education of the L.C.C. and of the Leeds, Nottingham, Bedford and Birmingham City Councils and Corporations. To all these and to many others I am deeply grateful.

Finally, I render thanks to the editor of *Punch* for his ideas and encouragement, respecting this glance at the lives and problems of all these newcomers. Like so many Jonahs, these adventurers have got into the belly of the British whale; but, unlike that ancient Hebrew prophet, it is unlikely that most of them will ever get out again. They have come to stay, and so, perhaps, the time has arrived for us to get to know them a little better.

BACK STREET NEW WORLDS

A Look at Immigrants in Britain

1. Refugees

ALONG with coal, steel, woolens, whisky, and pedigree bulls, for many years the British exported people. From vicarage, hamlet, and tenement there flowed a torrent of emigrants to the plains and prairies, mines and goldfields of various new worlds. Some seventeen million, it's believed, left between the Napoleonic Wars and World War I. On a reduced scale they're still going; about 127,000 left in 1962, mainly for Australia.

Today the covered wagon's gone into reverse. On balance, many more are coming to this man-packed island than are leaving it. In the back streets of industrial conurbations, in London's factories and Underground, in mills and transport services and foundries, immigrants now seek the opportunities the British looked for once in Saskatoon and Kimberley, the Murray River and the Canterbury plains. Pakistanis who go west come to Britain.

Way back into history, of course, from time to time Britain has received immigrants, whether they've been refugees from natural disasters, like the recent Tristan da Cunhans—who preferred volcanoes to hutted hostels in Surrey—or craftsmen like the Flemish weavers invited over by Edward III in 1337 "bringing their mystery with them"; and also asparagus, artichokes, and watercress, lilac from Turkey and the art of starching linen; or even occasional eccentrics who actually liked us, such as Henry James and Mr. T. S. Eliot.

In 1290, Edward I expelled the Jews, but Cromwell allowed them back again, and in 1956, British Jewry celebrated the tercentenary of their resettlement. Then came the Huguenots, our first minority of real significance in terms of size. After the St. Bartholomew's Day massacre in 1572 virtually the whole surviving population of Dieppe arrived in Rye and Winchelsea; many others came to southern England; it was a Huguenot wigmaker, Christopher Mountjoy, with whom Shakespeare lodged in Cripplegate in 1604.

Their renewed persecution by Louis XIV's dragoons, which began after the death of Cardinal Mazarin in 1661, aroused such sympathy in England that Charles II offered them sanctuary and promised freedom of worship, and the right to execute their skills and to educate their children. About 80,000 (a guess) came, out of a total of perhaps 350,000 who escaped the holocaust; something like half our quota, it is thought, subsequently re-emigrated. They started to make tapestries at Exeter, sails at Ipswich, beaver hats in Wandsworth, telescopes, biscuits, glass, and paper in various places, and above all, silk in the wastes of Spitalfields, which they beautified by means of gardens gay with tulips and dahlias, window boxes and ornamental pigeons. By 1718, London had thirty-one churches holding services in French, and a major export industry which thrived until so severely knocked by mechanization that in the mid-nineteenth century 30,000 silk weavers were unemployed.

Assimilation, held back at first by language and by religious observances, proceeded, on the whole, very smoothly,

and became virtually complete. A casebook example was provided by a Gascon who escaped to Holland and joined the
British Army, fought with distinction, gained promotion,
and was knighted by George II after the Battle of Dettingen.
He then sat as M.P. for Bath, entered the Privy Council, and
rose to become Commander in Chief of the Army—the first
professional soldier ever to do so, and a popular hero. This
was Lord Ligonier, who died at the age of ninety in 1770. (A
Huguenot it was who started Cheam preparatory school, of
recent fame; another, an F.R.S., invented a pressure cooker
and a precursor of the steam engine; others sired such families as Garrick, Romilly, Olivier, Layard, and Courtauld.)
Huguenots were welcomed, one of them recorded, with royal
munificence and public compassion; in 1719 only about
3,000 were "upon the list of those who enjoy public assistance," and the Queen was organizing sales of "little works
which she herself worked at and wore."

After the Huguenots there was a lull for over one and a
half centuries, ruffled but not really broken by the French
émigrés, about 40,000 of them, nearly all of whom subsequently returned to France. They gave rise to the first Aliens
Bill, of 1793, obliging foreigners to register. Various later,
nineteenth-century refugees from European tyrannies clus-
tered, according to *The Times,* round Leicester Square,
"wearing hats such as no one wears and hair where none
should be, a miserable, poverty-stricken, harassed population
who set all the powerful monarchs of Europe trembling except the Queen of England." Chronicling a halfway stage
towards assimilation, the Russian traveller Herzen commented, "They do not become English, but to some extent
cease to be German." That famous bearded pair, Marx and
Engels, were of their number.

2

The two major pressures that create refugees are tyranny and poverty. The latter was the cause of our next, greatest, and most persistent invasion: that of the Irish. The crest of this wave hit us during and after the potato famine. In 1846 some 280,000 starving Irish, destitute and ragged, many suffering from diseases and fevers, landed in Liverpool; in the year after, about 300,000.

There had always been quite a number of Irish around since the days of St. Patrick; even in 1413 they were considered to be such a nuisance that a statute had to be passed ordering "all Irishmen and Irish clerks, and beggars called chamberdekyns, to be voided out of the realm." In Cromwell's day they made more trouble by demonstrating against the public auction of women and children (white, not black) in the Bristol cattle market, where planters from Virginia and the West Indies came to bid. When the famine influx started, Britain already had about 400,000 Irish, rather more than 2 percent of the population. In addition seasonal harvesters came and went; a deck passage from Belfast to Glasgow cost fivepence, and this dropped, one year, to thruppence a head. By 1861 we had double the number—3 percent of the English population and nearly 7 of the Scottish. After that numbers fell until 1951. Everyone who possibly could went to America. Today we have over a million Irish-born in this country—many more, of course, of Irish origin—and they form by far our largest minority.

Packed into the slums of cities already overcrowded and horribly unsanitary, most of the famine refugees exchanged their peat-roofed hovels for heaps of rags in foul basements and bug-infested tenements, their few disease-blackened potatoes for stale bread, and the green fields and black bogs of County Cork or Connemara for the dank and grime-encrusted brick of Glasgow, Liverpool, and Leeds.

But they found work, at least if they were strong. This was the great age of canal and railway building, and the Irish navvies picked and shovelled thousands of miles of them. They moved about in "butty gangs," laying a tradition of footloose mobility that still persists, of fecklessness, adaptability, brawn, and drunkenness. A lot enlisted; by 1890 about three men in twenty in the Army were Irish. Others toiled as dockers, coal heavers, porters, sawyers, bricklayers, labourers—all the rough work, following the traditional pattern of the unskilled immigrant who gets the heaviest, dirtiest jobs the natives shun, and the accommodations from which they want to move away. A few were skilled, for instance linen weavers; there was even a sprinkling of shopkeepers, bankers, and lawyers, and more than a sprinkling of beggars. The women went into cotton mills and domestic service.

3

By the finish of the 1850s the famine flood was more or less over, and by the century's end it had dwindled to a trickle. But Irish immigration never ceased, and rose again at the time of the Troubles, especially after the United States fixed a quota in 1924, and in 1929 lowered it to less than 18,000 Irishmen a year.

Once more the Irish turned to Britain. Over 350,000 came to stay between 1946 and 1959. In London, by 1961, four people out of every hundred were Irish-born, compared with two Scots and two Welshmen. The Irish population of some Midland cities jumped by five or six times. (The spread of tractors in Ireland stimulated this movement; displaced Irish horse traders and tinkers came in search of new openings, mostly of a kind to employ sharp wits, easy tongues, and thirsty throats, rather than manual skills or the more solid citizenly virtues.)

Today Britain has more Irish-born people than the United States can muster, and the Irish fail to fill their American quota of less than 20,000 a year. Four out of every five live in our major cities and—unique among our minorities—there are more women than men. Some of these, no doubt, are here in search of mates, for the Irish have the highest proportion of bachelors in the world and more than one man in four never marries. Most of the male emigrants are under thirty, and Ireland is still being steadily drained of its young and vigorous citizens, despite the efforts of its government to reverse this trend.

Legally the Irish occupy a curious limbo of their own: they rank neither as Commonwealth citizens nor as aliens; no one knows exactly what they are. This, plus the permeable frontier between them and the Six Counties, enables them to bypass the Commonwealth Immigrants Act. This act does, however, provide machinery whereby they could be restricted should the British Government decide to rope them in. Unless it does, there is no prospect, writes Mr. John Jackson in his illuminating study, *The Irish in Britain,* of a decline in numbers of immigrants; for "the habit of emigration has become incorporated into Irish life," indeed, almost become a part of *rites de passage* for the young of both sexes. As for us, our construction industry and hospitals would starve but for Irish brawn and Irish readiness; and where would our drama be without its long tradition of Hibernian replenishment from Sheridan by way of Shaw and Synge to Sean O'Casey and Brendan Behan?

2. Tents of Israel

IN 1881, Tsar Alexander II of Russia was assassinated and the Jews were made scapegoats: pogroms of singular beastliness followed, and by 1905 over one million Jews had fled from Russia and Poland, mainly to the United States. Probably about 100,000 came to Britain, roughly doubling the existing Jewish population, then concentrated mainly in London, and spreading into northern cities such as Manchester, Leeds, Liverpool, and Glasgow. By 1914, Britain had 300,000 Jews; today, about 450,000, or just under 1 percent of our population. Well over half the world's Jews now live in the United States.

These Eastern European refugees brought with them no "mysteries" or skills, which in the ghettos they had not been allowed to learn or practice. They brought only themselves and their families—destitute, distraught, and often dirty; they packed into slums that the British, and even the Irish, were trying to quit, and settled into those few occupations that had been sanctioned in the ghetto: mainly street trading and tailoring. About one third, probably, became tailors in London's East End, in Leeds, and in Manchester; and the Jewish

stereotype of the sad-eyed, greasy-locked, rat-poor Yid stitch-
ing cross-legged in his ill-ventilated sweatshop came into being.

This Yiddish-speaking influx found the framework of a
much older Jewish community already in existence. In London the first synagogue, at Bevis Marks, had opened in 1701,
and a gradual process of emancipation from legal and religious disabilities had been completed in 1871 by an act ad-
mitting Jewish undergraduates to Oxford and Cambridge. By
then top Jews were snugly integrated: Rothschilds, Sassoons,
and Sebag-Montefiores had married into the British aristocracy, a Jew had been Prime Minister, and merchant bankers
in control of international finance owned Park Lane mansions, *objets d'art,* and race horses. Brighton had become a
town "three miles long and one yard wide with a Sassoon at
each end and one in the middle."

To such assimilated Jews this invasion from the ghettos can
scarcely have been welcome; even for the most integrated
anti-Semitism must always be a dog that only slumbers, never
dies. And many of the top British Jews belonged to a different order, the Sephardim, who had come from Spain and
Portugal as refugees from the Inquisition, and were known as
Marranos. (Elizabeth I's physician, Rodrigo Lopez, was
one.) They had spread a merchant's network over Western
Europe, kept out of trouble, formed a self-contained community, and prospered. These were the Jews that Cromwell
had recognized.

Later, and mainly as refugees from Cossack massacres in
Poland, came the first Jews of the Ashkenazim. For the most
part Yiddish-speaking, they formed a rougher, poorer, more
exotic community. The men wore beards and side curls,

cloaks and large hats, the women shaved their heads after marriage and wore wigs. Fagin was the stereotype. They had prospered sufficiently to oblige George II with a loan; in return, Parliament in 1753 granted them the right to naturalization. This excited so much popular resentment that the bill had to be withdrawn. The slogan "No Jews, no wooden shoes" struck a glancing blow at the Huguenots—no immigrants, in fact—and expressed, it is said, the last popular outburst of anti-Semitism in Britain, until Mosley marched through London's East End. The influx of the eighties greatly reinforced the Ashkenazim, who already outnumbered the Sephardim by five or six to one.

So large an invasion of such very alien Eastern Europeans might well have led to trouble in the eighties; however, the established Jews behaved with characteristic generosity and the natives with their customary restraint. "If five shipwrecked Jews reach a desert island, there'll soon be six synagogues, seven rabbis, and eight wardens," is a Jewish saying. So *chevras,* the nuclei of churches, developed into synagogues, schools opened, kosher butchers multiplied, Yiddish newspapers circulated, burial groups thrived, and that nexus of charitable bodies with which the Jews support their own kind cast its protective web around the whole transplanted community.

In (historically speaking) a remarkably short time the refugees had branched out into other trades and professions, entered the universities, bought property, spread out from the slums, and gone a long way towards full integration into British life. Both Britain and the Jews had a breathing space of about fifty years before the next influx. This was not nearly such a large one, it concentrated mainly on London and it was without doubt, in terms of intellect and skill, the

most valuable batch of immigrants since the Huguenots.
These were the refugees from Hitler, of whom about 60,000
came to Britain up to 1939.

2

Unlike that of all other minorities, the Jewish birthrate is
lower than the national average—not a lot, but enough to
matter. No one knows why. Making up in quality what they
lack in bulk, nearly three times as many Jewish students enter universities as would be the case if they conformed to the
national average. Less than 1 percent of the total population
is Jewish but nearly 5 percent of the fellows of the Royal
Society. Genes? Or a stronger tradition of respect for learning
than our own, plus a long sharpening of wits on the grind-
stone of persecution? Again, no one knows.

Intermarriage is, of course, the main social mechanism for
digesting minorities. Just how many Jews marry out of their
community isn't known; it is on the increase, certainly. The
best guess seems to be that somewhere between one quarter
and one third of Jewish men pick Gentile brides, but that
Jewish women stick much closer to their kind, with only
between one tenth and one fifth marrying "out," and about
the same proportion staying single. The marriage rate at synagogues had dropped from ten to four per thousand in the last
sixty years—it is now only half the national average, which
has remained fairly constant for the last half century.

This trend, if it continues, must gradually obliterate the
Jews as a separate community. And the further it goes, the

faster the pace, if conclusions reached by Dr. L. Rosenberg in Canada can be generally applied. Montreal has about 100,000 Jews, of whom 3.7 percent marry "out." In Winnipeg some 20,000 Jews have an intermarriage rate of 6.5 percent; and of Vancouver's small community of 7,000 Jews, 26.3 percent marry Gentiles. The smaller the community, the higher the rate of intermarriage, which is only natural; Dr. Rosenberg has worked out that a community of 7,000 would, by the time factors such as age, height, intelligence, and income had whittled down the choice, offer any given young man only twelve potential mates—not enough, apparently; he turns his roving eye on Gentiles. Somewhere around this 7,000 mark seems to be the lower limit of viability.

All this begs the question "What is a Jew?", another to which there can be no clear-cut answer. "Every child of a Jewess is a Jew," I was told—they are a martrilineal race; but every child of intermarriage does not wish to be one. The only practical definition seems to be that anyone is a Jew who thinks of himself as one and who maintains a link, however tenuous, with some aspect of Jewish faith, tradition, or organized body.

Of these membership in a burial society has the most significance. A man may never enter a synagogue all his life, even on the Day of Atonement, but still intend to lay his bones in a Jewish cemetery. That classifies him as a Jew. Following the same pattern, the first corporate act of our newest minority, the Muslims, has been to buy a piece of burial ground in Birmingham or Bermondsey or Smethwick.

A strong hard core of Orthodox Jewish zealots attempts to resist the total assimilation of the Jews. They wish their community, while fitting into its surroundings, to maintain its heart intact. British Jewry supports an astonishingly large number of bodies and organizations whose object is to keep alive this sense of community, both by promoting Jewish culture and religion and by caring for all needy, distressed, or handicapped co-racialists who slip through the meshes of the welfare state. For this latter purpose the Jewish Board of Guardians, with its branches in all major cities, is the principal channel; for the former, the synagogue and Talmud Torah classes in the schools, which provide instruction in the Hebrew faith and tongue. The Board of Deputies of British Jews is the official body that speaks for British Jewry, protects its interests, and acts as its connecting link with the government.

3

Leeds has the third-largest Jewish community in Britain, exceeded only by London and Manchester. (The Jews are the most urban of people; over eight out of every ten live in our six largest cities, nearly two thirds in Greater London.) The number of Jews in Leeds has doubled in the last sixty years and now stands at about 20,000 out of a population of some 515,000. This is about 3.5 percent, or more than three times the national average.

In Leeds about 5,500 Jewish families support some 120 different organizations, including eleven synagogues with a combined membership of 4,200 families. Thus three Jews in four belong to synagogues. In this they do much better than the Christians, of whom, in the country generally, about one in ten is a regular churchgoer.

For the rest, there is a bevy of bodies: housing associations and workers' co-operatives, a home for aged Jews and a Board of Shechita to supervise ritual slaughter for kosher meat; convalescent homes and youth centres, ex-servicemen's associations and friendship clubs; meal services for the elderly, an orchestral society, a marriage club, a Zionist group; fellowships and lodges, centres and study groups, missions and guilds—everything to ensure that, as the organizer of the Jewish Representative Council (which gathers them all under one umbrella) put it, "No Jew need ever be in want, and not only physically—nor look to Gentiles for charity."

Here is the story of a Leeds Jew, a respected citizen, typical of many others. His grandfather fled from a Russian ghetto to settle in the slums of the Leylands, where Jews were already established with a synagogue opened in the 1840s. Established, but not welcomed; signs reading "No Jews need apply" were common, and at weekends groups of young hooligans armed with cudgels would invade the Leylands, then virtually a ghetto, to beat up any Jews they could corner. His father, born in Chapeltown (a little farther out), married an English Jewess; their family grew up to hear little spoken but Yiddish, to see Yiddish signs in all the shops, to attend the synagogue and Talmud Torah classes regularly, to shun contamination with food that might be ritually impure.

Their eldest son has moved from Chapeltown to one of the middle-class, prosperous suburbs, that of Moortown, whose golf club, with a membership, predominantly Jewish, of 700, commands a subscription of over one hundred pounds a year. In Chapeltown today you don't see a single Yiddish sign; as for the provision shops, instead of Levi and Jacobs there are Singh, Ahmed, and Patel; the West Indians, Pakistanis, and Indians have taken over as the Jews moved out. The one

surviving synagogue in the Leylands area, which the Jews of
Leeds had intended to preserve as a symbol and memorial, is
now to be demolished under the corporation's redevelop-
ment plans.

The only grandson of this Jewish family practices law in an
almost Jewless Yorkshire town and gets his kosher food sent
out from Leeds. One of his sisters went to Israel, worked on a
kibbutz, married, and emigrated to America; the other married a Jewish businessman in Britain. All are raising their
families as Jews, but whether the children will grow up to
keep the custom is another matter. Among most of the young
there is a noticeably diminished enthusiasm for Jewish practices. "Jews," one of them told me, "are becoming part of
their background; I'm a Jew, but I'm also a Yorkshireman;
sometimes I can hardly bring myself to open the Yorkshire
Post in case there's been a county championship disaster."
After some initial resistance Leeds can be said to have taken
the Jews to its bosom, and in 1941 elected its first Jewish
Lord Mayor.

Not only have Jews dispersed first from the Leylands, then
to Chapeltown, and now to other parts of the city, they've
moved away from tailoring and street trading into nearly all
the modern occupations of mankind. It was a Jew, Herman
Friend, who virtually started the mass production of cheap
clothing after a Gentile colleague, John Barran, had invented
the band knife that cut cloth in bulk. Leeds remains the
centre of this trade, now enormously refined and expanded,
and harbours the largest ready-made clothing business in the
world. Although this firm remains under Jewish management, out of a labour force of over 6,000 in Leeds only about
250 are estimated now to be identifiable Jews. At the Feast of
the Passover this firm makes special arrangements in the can-

teen for the Orthodox, who must eat off separate crockery; the number making use of them was down to ninety last year.

Now there are Jewish doctors and lawyers, magistrates and aldermen; hairdressers, electricians, salesmen, secretaries, butchers, bakers, and candlestick makers, and all the rest. Insofar as generalizations can be made, one is that Jews tend to concentrate on the distributive, clothing, retail, and catering trades and to be thinner on the ground in such pursuits as construction work and heavy engineering; a second, that about three times more Jews than Gentiles set up in business on their own. A tailoring tradition survives; Jewish membership in the National Union of Tailors and Garment Workers is fifteen times as high as it would be to match the proportion of Jews in our total population.

4

Apart from the synagogue, the focal point in Leeds of Jewish efforts to preserve and perpetuate their culture lies in the Talmud Torah classes in the schools. In Leeds the Talmud Torah Hebrew Education Board organizes evening classes at six branches and "withdrawal classes" at twenty of the city's schools; for these either the pupils are "withdrawn" from normal studies for two or three periods a week or they attend special classes on Saturdays. Out of an estimated 2,700 Jewish schoolchildren (in round figures) about 1,600 attend these classes. Some of the nonattenders are below school age; even so, that leaves a pretty sizable gap—part of the steady and quickening erosion process that eats away at the community.

Only about half the Jewish children make use of a kosher meal service provided in the school canteens. (Animals must be killed by a method known as *shechita*, the severing of all veins and arteries in the neck with a single knife stroke, in obedience to a divine command against consuming blood; only Jews of proved morality who have been trained, licensed, and certified by the ecclesiastical authority may carry out the ritual.) Only about one British Jew in three, it has been estimated, now insists on kosher food. This does not necessarily mean that both the others have abandoned their faith. They may belong to Reform synagogues, whose members are the nonconformists of the Hebrew religion.

But nowadays many of the young are drifting away from the synagogue, and from the strict religious observances which forbade their grandmothers to cook so much as a potato on the Sabbath and obliged the poorest Jewish family to hire a Gentile girl to lay a Sabbath fire. (Even today the *really* strict ones won't turn on the electricity.) In Leeds, I heard a Gentile health visitor remark, "I live in a Jewish area, and there's scarcely a day goes by I don't get a whiff of bacon; that's a smell you *can't* conceal."

The Jews of Leeds have followed the pattern to which almost every wave of immigrants, anywhere, conforms. First they made for that part of the city which already had a nucleus of Jews. This process is made easier by the natives, who, when large numbers of foreigners and strangers move in, generally try to move out. Property then deteriorates in value, and this gives the immigrants a chance to find living space at prices they can scrape together. So a Jewish quarter—or a quarter predominantly Italian or Greek, Polish or Pakistani, Jamaican or Sikh—springs up. This isn't a result of design or policy, as ghettos were; it's a natural progression of events.

Gradually the newcomers adjust, dig in, work, save, and thrive. They start to stratify, as sociologists have it; some rise in the world to form or join a middle class. The first social action of this successful top layer is generally to move away from the close-packed slum in which they found a footing and to buy better-class property farther out. This centrifugal movement tends to disperse them, physically and culturally alike; in both senses they often leave the synagogue behind. In Leeds, for example, a focal point was the Jewish Institute, founded in Chapeltown "to provide healthy recreation by means of lectures, debates, concerts, athletics, etc." Reflecting the Jewish exodus from Chapeltown, as well perhaps as changing outlooks, its membership dropped from 2,600 in 1948 to 1,500 ten years later. So the very success of the Jews (or of any minority) at once reduces their concentration, increases their dilution, and accelerates the rate of their absorption into the community.

5

If you drift away from the faith, eat bacon, learn no Hebrew, even marry a Gentile, then what keeps you a Jew? It's not even as if the physical stamp were constant or predictable.

"A Jew can't get rid of his feelings of generosity and resentment," one suggested. "When I was a boy—we were down at the very bottom in a Chapeltown slum—every Sabbath morning my mother made a pile of six pennies and counted them out in front of me. 'That's for the Board of Guardians; this for the hospital; that for the school . . .' She did this to teach me, and I've never forgotten. We Jews pay our taxes like everyone else, contribute to charity, and on top of that support a whole network of our own organizations—an umbrella we hold over ourselves.

"Then there's our family feeling, our sense of kinship— that's another of our traits. It's very strong. A Jew would rather go short of luxuries than see his children deprived of their mother, however good the nursery school." Statistically only 11 percent of Jewish wives work for wages as against 34 percent of wives in the country as a whole.

Jews observe a stricter moral code than most Gentiles do. This is hard to prove, but fewer juveniles appear to go astray among the Jewish than the non-Jewish community. Murder and rape are said to be rare, and there is relatively little drunkenness.

In Leeds the Jewish divorce rate is only half that of the national average. Probably these virtues arise less from innate godliness than from greater family cohesion, the tighter hold of a stern religion, and racial pride—"What will the Goyim say?" Nor are Jews, as a group, without their weaknesses: if there are fewer than average drunks there are probably more gamblers, and if Jews are less likely to batter you to death with a blunt instrument they are more likely to fiddle their taxes.

"Anglo-Jewry is biologically on the decline." This is the conclusion reached by Dr. Maurice Freedman in his study *A Minority in Britain*. The average size of Jewish families has fallen below the replacement rate, so, unless the trend is reversed or another wave of immigration arrives, a slow extinction can only be a matter of time. "Little may be left that is distinctively Jewish."

For most Jews this is an emotional tragedy, and yet it is a measure of achievement—the achievement of their own adaptability and of British tolerance. For the British *have* been tolerant; despite a few lapses, probably more tolerant than any other nation on earth. Britain was the only country in Europe where the number of Jews went up, not down, between 1939 and 1950—by 40 percent. "The storm of destruction passed over Europe," Dr. Freedman comments, "but left the Jews in Britain intact. Indeed, in a stronger position." There has, of course, been Mosley, and latterly Colin Jordan; a number of clubs or societies still won't take in Jews, but the vast British majority rejected, and continue to reject, overt anti-Semitism. Out of the Mosley episode came the Council of Christians and Jews, a high-level attempt in terms of dignitaries of both churches to draw the taproot of anti-Semitism—the casting of the Jews as scapegoats for the Crucifixion.

The attitude of British Jews towards Israel is a pointer. Zionism is a cup of compensation—pie not in the sky but in the dish, for people who've never had any pie. The deeper your own frustration, the more the land of Zion means to you. The converse holds true. If you have a home already and a tolerable future, you don't need a *kibbutz* in the sands of the Negev. Israel has attracted fewer settlers from Britain than from any other major European country—probably less than 7,000 or 8,000 between its inception and the present day. Now the flow has dwindled to a trickle of trained professionals like engineers, teachers, doctors, and pharmacists—plus one fashion designer, one optician, and one French translator in a recent batch of emigrants. Last year about 800 left Britain for Israel, but some of these may return.

Of all our minorities the Jews are, in sociological jargon, the most "upwardly mobile"; feet well planted on the social escalator, Whitechapel and Stepney lie behind. (Before the war roughly 100,000 Jews lived in these two boroughs; today, probably less than 15,000.) Today it's Stamford Hill and Hackney, leading on to Hampstead and Golders Green. The Jews, writes Dr. Ernest Krausz (himself a Rumanian immigrant), are fast becoming a "green-belt society," and "keeping up with the Cohens is a more taxing business than keeping up with the Joneses."

They are, in fact, committing voluntary self-genocide, the fate of all minorities who successfully integrate. Dr. Krausz makes the point that because they are the most urbanized of modern communities, they are (as American students say) "the most likely to succeed." Acquisitive, adaptable, alert, quick-witted, pushing, industrious, at once sensitive and ruthless, sentimental and tough, clannish and extrovert, "the Jew has become the prototype of the twentieth-century man in Western society." Today the tents of Jewry are pitched on Stamford Hill.

3. Poles to Dinner

CAUGHT in a wave of tatterdemalion soldiery washed up on our shores after the fall of France in 1940 were over 27,000 Poles. These were forerunners of the much greater influx that arrived in 1946 under the command of General Wladyslaw Anders, the residue of one and half million Poles whom the Russians had uprooted from their native soil and deported in cattle trucks to the U.S.S.R.

In 1941, when Hitler's armies invaded the Soviet Union, these uprooted Poles underwent, in Russian eyes, a magic transformation: they were changed overnight from prisoners of war and forced labour into gallant allies to be recruited for the anti-Nazi struggle. From them was formed the Polish Second Corps, or Anders' army.

Despite their common cause with the Soviets, few of this army's stalwarts had a soft spot for the U.S.S.R., or indeed for much else; they were a tough lot of men who fought, with a spirit proper to Poles, in Palestine and Italy, and reached Britain, some 100,000 strong, when the kill was over. Others came later: escaped conscripts from the Wehrmacht, prisoners of war from German camps, political prisoners, and the

like, none of whom at first doubted that he was on his way
home to his native land.

When the Communists gobbled up the whole of Poland,
nothing remained for Anders' men but a hard core of belief
that one day a Polish phoenix would be reborn to spread its
wings. Meanwhile most of them chose freedom and exile; the
Poles had come to dinner in a big way. Later about 10,000
left, mainly for the United States, Canada, and Australia.

Those who stayed were placed by the Polish Resettlement
Corps in Nissen-hutted camps where they were fed, sheltered,
and sent forth to their employment, until gradually they
fitted themselves into British life. This took time. There are
still one or two hostels left to house a residue of old and
infirm.

Meanwhile the wives and families of some of Anders' men
arrived. The saga of their trek on foot from central and eastern Russia to the Caspian Sea and down to the Persian Gulf
is a fantastic epic. Some of them ended up in such unlikely
spots as central Tanganyika and western Uganda. Only the
tough survived, and tough they were. When at last they
reached Britain they seemed to their more sophisticated fellow countrymen a wild, uncouth bunch, soon to be reinforced by several thousands, no less battered, from the European displaced persons camps.

Their Church—nearly all were Roman Catholics—their
own voluntary welfare services, and their involuntary hosts
got busy and, like beneficial earthworms bent on drawing
roughage into the soil, worked them gradually, family by
family and man by man, into the fabric of British life. This
process was hastened by intermarriage with the natives, especially those of Scotland, where Anders' army was based during and immediately after the war.

2

Our Polish minority today stands at around 130,000, including about 16,000 children born here and so technically not immigrants, and those who have been naturalized. About 95,000 Poles have not, perhaps because they still dream of ending their days in Poland. Some ten million Poles live outside Poland, compared with about thirty million in the homeland. Like all groups of political refugees, the British minority is aging and not being replenished.

One in ten of those who passed through the Resettlement Corps came equipped with a higher education. Of some 102,000 Poles nearly 2,500 had formerly been civil servants and about 2,750 members of the so-called liberal professions, such as teachers, doctors, architects, and journalists (over 130 of them). There were no less than 850 former lawyers, and nearly 500 classified as writers and artists. (The journalists and writers seem to have been kept separate.) Also included were some 1,100 qualified engineers and over 7,300 skilled technicians.

Seldom can a minority have arrived *en bloc* carrying such a high proportion of trained, educated, and presumably useful people and so few of *hoi polloi*. As for the social status of the new arrivals, over 6,000 former farmers and landowners came and only 2,500 farmhands—a very different story from Russian Jews fleeing from pogroms or Irish peasants from famine, but comparable, possibly, with Flemings and Huguenots. On the other hand, many of these Poles were middle-aged, found new ways hard to learn, failed to get a start in their true professions, and both economically and socially came down in the world. Nevertheless, there are thought to be about 600 Polish doctors and 80 dentists practicing in Britain, and about 2,000 engineers and technicians. And over 10,000 younger Poles have trained, with government grants, in various skills and professions.

Their first objective was a job, and after that a house of their own. With patience, doggedness, and acumen they set out to acquire them, and today almost every settled Pole, except the very old and a few total failures, is a householder. Because, when they first arrived, the government placed them and their families in camps and hostels, they were spared the free-for-all in which the more recent West Indian and Asian arrivals have been so painfully embroiled; they could search for living space more or less at leisure, and ease their way in.

After, or with, a house they wanted economic independence. The range and number of businesses these exiles have started is remarkable. The Polish trade directory for 1963 classifies occupations in London alone under 218 different heads. There's scarcely a pie in the country without a Polish finger in it somewhere. Not all, of course, are beneficial; Rachman was a Polish Jew.

The trade directory lists independent Polish businesses in 142 British towns, from Cupar and Montrose in Scotland to Holyhead in Anglesey (hotel), Saxmundham in Suffolk (mushroom farm), Lampeter in Cardigan (Catholic club) and Mildord Haven (groceries). While Poles have scattered everywhere, they're mainly metropolitan, and have set up over 1,000 businesses in London as against 600 plus in the rest of the British Isles. The Union of Polish Merchants and

Industrialists believe there to be some 2,500 separate Polish businesses. Probably at least one third of all the Poles in Britain have become Londoners, with Birmingham, Manchester, and Bradford next. Poles run fifty-three separate concerns in Edinburgh (the services and firms include hotels, pharmacies, engineering, delicatessens, bakeries, watchmakers, tailors, hairdressers, leather goods, photographers, and one gift shop, builder, printer, stamp dealer, wool shop, advertising agency and upholsterer), and only two in Liverpool.

3

Like other immigrants, the Poles went first where they could squeeze in cheaply, in London to poorer districts like Paddington and Lambeth. As they got on in the world, they moved out into areas more middle class in *ethos,* and today the focus, insofar as one exists, is South Kensington, where Earl's Court Road is still remembered as the Polish Corridor.

For its size the Polish community maintains a vast number of organizations to cater to social, spiritual, and economic needs. The oldest, and still at the core of Poland-in-exile, is the Ex-Combatants' Association—*Stowarzyszenie Polskich Kombatantow,* or the S.P.K.—with branches in most major British cities and headquarters in South Kensington.

At its peak the membership was 15,000, but now it is down to 11,000 and gradually shrinking. Some younger people join, but not many; lately its officers have been trying to widen its appeal by developing the welfare side. The S.P.K.

maintains, for example, a wing of a hospital at Dartford, Kent, for the treatment of mental cases, where all the doctors and nurses are Poles. The elders' efforts to hold a new generation of the British-born centres round the Polish-language Saturday schools, of which there are now over sixty, run by voluntary effort and by the parish priests. They are well attended, but probably don't reach more than about one fifth of the children, most of whom are growing up with little knowledge of the Polish tongue.

The religious tie is more powerful. The network of Polish Catholic parishes is nationwide, with a Vicar-General in London at the centre and a focal church at Ealing, nearly always packed for Sunday Mass. Upwards of 2,000 Poles assemble annually at St. Mary's, Clapham, for the Corpus Christi procession; in every city with a sizable Polish community one or other of the Roman Catholic churches is put at the disposal of the Polish priest for well-attended weekly Masses. This is an effective means of holding the young, and other methods reinforce it; for instance, Polish troops of Scouts and Guides, and youth and sports clubs.

4

Of the younger generation a sizable proportion is the progeny of Polish husbands and British wives. How much store do these half Poles set by their Polish heritage? Two tendencies pull in opposite ways. On the one hand, there's the tendency to conform, strongly reinforced by natural human idleness. It's much less trouble just to be British. On the other, there is the urge to be different, and to weave some strands of colour into the subfusc fabric of daily urban life.

In one family I sampled, typical perhaps of one kind of Pole, both the Anglo-Polish schoolgirls were proud of their Slavic blood, belonged to a Polish troop of Guides, and when younger had learned Polish dances, which they'd performed in traditional dresses made by their mother, a Scot from Dundee. Now they attend the Saturday classes, know (their father says) more Polish history than he does, and are saving for a trip to Poland when they leave school.

These girls are typical, however, of only one kind of Polish situation; their father was a cavalry officer and a landowner; now he's a factory hand in a big engineering works, paying off a loan for his semi-detached house. Most of the fellow Poles in his community came from a peasant background, or were workingmen. Shrewder than he is, he said, and more frugal, they prosper more; they buy crates of poultry at knock-down prices when the market's glutted and make a bit at weekends by dressing them and hawking them around as oven-ready birds. Few of their children attend Saturday schools or sustain their Polishness. The children, given no incentive to do otherwise, want to blend. Partly, no doubt, this is because their Polish tongue is something of a *patois*— less a source of pride than a class distinction they have thrown off and want to forget. At any rate, the parents don't encourage their children to learn it. With the language Polish culture, too, will fade and die.

Several Polish publications go the rounds. Once there were over two hundred; now there's only one daily newspaper, *Dziennik Polski,* one bi-weekly, four or five weeklies, and several monthly journals, mainly cultural and religious. There are several Polish presses in London, and standards of production are high; I saw a beautifully produced Polish translation of *The Iliad* printed there. The circulation of the daily reached its peak of over 30,000 in 1951, then started to decline. Nevertheless, it survives to link Poles in Britain not only with one another but with exiled Poles elsewhere.

5

In October 1956 deep and prolonged discontent forced the Polish Government, without open revolt (as in Hungary), to concede profound political changes. There was a great relaxation in the Polish homeland, a big thaw. Censorship mellowed, restrictions were lifted, people breathed an air if not free at least a great deal more open, permissive, and invigorating than before.

In the next four years over 30,000 Poles were granted visas to visit British relatives and friends. Many exiled Poles, those at least with British passports, felt that at long last they could visit their homes. Since then there has been a constant coming and going between Britain and Poland. This has worked towards maintaining, or restoring, a sense of Polishness among the exiles. The umbilical cord, as it were, has been at least partially restored. Young people reared in England have visited grandparents hitherto but names; their counterparts from Poland have come to Britain, some have even married British Poles.

London's *Dziennik Polski* sometimes carries advertisements from girls in Poland, where there is a surplus of women, for British mates. Alas, when they get them, not all are satisfied. Poles reared in Britain have, it seems, taken on protective colouring distasteful to the native Polish temperament. Disillusioned Polish-reared wives complain that British Poles are miserly, dour, selfish, and given to evenings out with men friends swilling beer. Whereas a lot of British Poles go over to their homeland for a holiday, very few decide to stay.

For nearly twenty years the prime object of the Poles in exile, next to winning a livelihood, has been to resist integration. While not wishing to be looked down upon as aliens, nor to quarrel with their hosts, Poles would prefer not to be swallowed. "We don't want to be sunk in the British community," one of them said. They're like the goat inside a boa constrictor determined to resist the reptile's digestive juices and maintain a whole skin.

Can this be done? The Jews think so. "I've got a dual loyalty," one said. "I don't find that this presents any difficulty. I'm an Englishman and loyal to my country. I'm also a Jew and loyal to Jewish values. These are cultural and religious. There's no conflict."

Poles also believe that they can keep alive their language, read Polish newspapers and journals, celebrate Independence Day in November and Emancipation Day in May, teach their children Polish dances and songs, take part in Polish Masses and Corpus Christi processions, eat Polish food, without violating any British loyalty. Both Poles and Jews have a homeland to look to for spiritual refreshment, one in bondage and the other free. Poles still believe—or say they do—that this bondage will end. "Not revolution," one said, "God forbid; evolution. It's bound to come." This faith has survived so many centuries and persecutions, it must be indestructible by now.

It does not seem impossible to operate a dual loyalty, one to a cultural deity, the other to a national Caesar. From the host's point of view minorities can nourish and enrich, as they always have. Instead of the goat and the boa constrictor one can use the simile of the segments of an orange, each distinct and yet wrapped in one skin. But to resist the tremendous pressures of the modern world towards conformity, stronger than ever before, calls for an effort of the communal will that may be too much even for the national ardour and endurance of the Poles. About the only survival of Huguenot apartheid seems to be a provision for the preaching of a sermon in French at Rochester in Kent once a year, on the fourth Wednesday in June.

4. Negroes Next Door

I THINK it hit me most in Bath; that elegant, essentially European eighteenth-century town with its honey-coloured crescents and its ghosts of fobs and beaux and Jane Austen and the stout, ebony Jamaican in her baggy purple cardigan and red beret and old skirt, pushing a pram over a zebra crossing while Negro labourers slouched along the pavement in their muddied working clothes. There are many places where you'll see many more dark faces, but somehow they don't look quite so alien against a background that's more drab and nondescript, less patently English, than this memorial to a pre-industrial age.

And yet in Bath's heyday to see a Negro page in hose and doublet carrying the fan of a pomaded lady stepping forth from a sedan chair was a sight as commonplace as gouty gentlemen. Sometimes the pages wore silver collars and were pampered like pet dogs. Girls, too, were employed; Pepys had a Negro cookmaid who "dressed the meat mighty well." They belonged to the first sizable colored minority in Britain, slaves brought over in the eighteenth century and pronounced free by Lord Mansfield in his famous judgment in 1772. Few, if any, returned to their native lands, and in time

they vanished as completely as a conjurer's rabbit—biologically absorbed into the mainstream of Anglo-Saxon pallor.
There are thought to have been about 15,000 of them.

After that there was a lull, except for coloured seamen, who
settled in such spots as Cardiff's Tiger Bay, and for a few
students, until World War II, when batches of West Indians
were brought over to work in factories and others joined the
R.A.F. This started the movement which grew into the influx
which caused all the bother and resulted in the Commonwealth Immigrants Act.

Most of the airmen, like the pages, stayed on when their
time was up, or else went home, spread word of good jobs and
pay, collected spouses, and returned to Britain. The word
went around, and people from overcrowded Caribbean islands, where jobs were few and prospects meagre, began to
emigrate to our own overcrowded islands, where jobs were
open and material prospects fair, even if skies were grey and
the natives not overfriendly. A great impetus was given in
1952 when the United States, by passing the McCarran Act,
virtually shut its doors to West Indians, and Britain became
the only remaining wide-open territory for emigrants.

At first it was a trickle; in 1951 we still had only about
15,000 West Indians. It soon speeded up. Between the end of
World War II and the coming into force of the Commonwealth Immigrants Act on July 1, 1962, just over one million
immigrants arrived here from various Commonwealth countries and from Southern Ireland. We've become so used to
the Irish coming and going—mostly coming—that we scarcely
think of them as immigrants, but they form much the largest
single group. Thirty-nine out of every hundred of our postwar immigrants were Irish, and altogether about 400,000
have stayed. (In addition we have, in round figures, about

half a million aliens.) Then come the West Indians: just over twenty-four out of every hundred. At least two thirds of these are Jamaicans.

In all about 263,700 West Indians are reckoned to have moved over here during those sixteen years. Most of them left their families behind, and the womenfolk and children are following now, or will soon follow, so the numbers are sure to go on rising. It has been said—a guess, of course—that 100,000 children have been left behind in Jamaica alone and 150,000 in the Caribbean generally. They won't all follow, but many of them will. In the first full year since the act (July 1962– July 1963) nearly seven out of every ten arrivals from the Caribbean were women and children, who bypass the restrictions. In the last year before the act came into force, we took over 62,000 Caribbeans; this dropped to 10,000 or so, but now it is rising again. In the last three months of 1963 the net inflow of Caribbeans was just about 4,000. From all quarters we gained over 30,000 immigrants, on average 330 a day— nearly as many as during the whole of the previous year.

Nearly all West Indian men come under their own steam, almost always to a friend or relative already here. They share his room until they find their own. Each West Indian becomes a nucleus around which others gather, a spore; once started off, the process gathers speed very rapidly. Groups originating not merely in a certain island, say Jamaica or Trinidad, or even in a certain town or district, but in one particular parish or village, tend to transplant themselves to one particular borough, district, or even street at the other end. Thus you may find twenty or thirty families from a single parish in Jamaica clustering together in a couple of streets in Notting Hill or Brixton or Birmingham or Leeds.

This makes for coziness and security from the immigrant's point of view; he brings part of his environment along, even if he has to leave the sunshine and some of the children. It doesn't make for integration, by any means.

2

A roof, a job, a woman—three primary needs of male mankind. Bedded down for the time being with Uncle Oswald or Cousin Deborah, the newcomer must look around for a place of his own, where he can bring his family. Now his troubles really begin. In this, of course, he's simply sharing our trouble, the trouble of the host community. We're all in this together, as the waiting lists of every housing authority in the country show.

The housing situation is a jungle, but the basic facts are plain. Despite the addition of some 300,000 new dwellings annually—the government's target is now 350,000—we are not keeping pace with the overall demand. Our numbers are mounting, both by natural increase and by immigration, pretty smartly; up by about three million in the last decade. (Another eight million are expected in the next two decades.) Our present increase is mopping up annually about 125,000 of our 300,000 new dwellings. More than that, our rate of "household forming" is going up by leaps and bounds —17 percent in the same period.

"Household forming" rises faster than the population for various reasons: people live longer, and so more dwellings are needed for the elderly; they marry younger and want to set up on their own; above all, the affluent society leads them to expect different and superior types of houses or flats.

Of the seventeen million houses on this island nearly half were built before 1919, and of these a majority have become, or are becoming, obsolete. Nearly three million of them have stood for more than a century. The official estimate that 600,000 actual slum dwellings are due for demolition is almost certainly an underestimate.

All this adds up to a really staggering task, to be tackled by an industry which, in terms of organization and imagination, is on the whole archaic, chronically short of skilled labour, ill managed and undercapitalized, mostly split into little family firms or partnerships employing less than twenty men, and faced with enormous demands apart from housing—roads, schools, power stations, new towns, universities. It's a wonder the immigrants aren't all living in bus shelters or tents.

What they have done, by and large, is to move into houses from which the natives want to move out. This doesn't necessarily mean—though it does sometimes—into slums. I have seen immigrants living in revolting slums in Stepney, Balsall Heath in Birmingham, and elsewhere, but far more in substantial Victorian houses, with names like Blenheim Villas and Cadogan Mansions, in Leeds, Bradford, Birmingham, and Southall, as well as in London. These are the sorts of houses that would once have had a maid-of-all-work in the attic, a mistress in her decent bombazine mending pinafores in the parlour, and the master in his striped trousers, black coat, and wing collar going off to his city office every morning on the dot.

Almost everywhere the pattern's been the same: into these middle-class, nineteenth-century houses, maybe with a little front garden and a yard at the back, go the immigrants, often with broods as ample as their predecessors had. They buy Victoriana because they get it cheap and because it suits them. They get such houses cheap because they are too big for a single family these days, cannot be readily or economically converted into flats, and are rent-controlled. When a single room falls vacant, immigrants snap up the whole property.

To live hugger-mugger with one room for each family and plenty of communal life within the larger interrelated group —the extended family—is just what they were used to back home and what many of them like. What the natives are discarding the immigrants are picking up, at first at bargain prices; though where racketeers have cottoned on to this, as in west London, bargains have vanished. This particular form of property racket seems to be confined mainly to London; at least you don't hear so much about it in the Midlands and the North. There immigrants have bought slum houses, but still habitable houses, for two or three hundred pounds.

3

If there's one thing on which all immigrants agree it is that, almost to a man, they mean to buy a house; and to this end they save and save and save. A house represents the very thing they've left home to find—security. In some groups—notably most Italians, Indians, and Pakistanis—to save is second nature anyway; in others, notably the Caribbeans, it's apt to go against the grain. Most West Indians are spenders by nature. Nevertheless, to get a house a great many of them *do* save. On top of this they send money home. Between 1954 and 1960 at least two and a half million pounds were remitted to Barbados and nearly seventeen million to Jamaica, through the post office alone.

In Birmingham some 5,000 houses are now owned by coloured immigrants, of whom there are about 70,000 plus in the city—just over 6 percent of the population. Of this coloured group some 40,000—between half and two thirds—are West Indians, but they haven't managed to buy more than about one fifth of the houses that have passed into coloured ownership; most of the rest have gone to Indians and Pakistanis. They're the ones who *really* save.

More and more the housing pattern is coming to be an Indian or Pakistani landlord letting rooms to West Indians, Pakistanis, and whites. The whites are often Irish, who very seldom manage to save and in any case are generally too fidgety to tie themselves to property. Like their coloured fellow immigrants, most of them are at the bottom of the economic ladder, and tend to be less fussy about other peoples' habits than the English are, less set in their ways. A footnote to the colour question came the other day from a Pakistani in Bradford who put up a sign, White Tenants Only, on his door.

He must have had some jaundicing experience, because most landlords seem to find West Indians satisfactory tenants in at least two important ways: prompt with the rent, and clean—at least inside their own apartments. "I've never yet been inside a dirty West Indian room," a health visitor told me. "The women are nearly always scrupulously clean and their children beautifully cared for—better than among our own people, by and large."

A nurse who looks after the health of women workers in a factory remarked, "I've yet to come across a dirty Jamaican girl; their underwear is spotless however much they're caught unawares; whereas some of the whites . . ." West Indians are not only clean in their persons, but healthy; you scarcely ever see an undernourished specimen. The men are often strapping, and the women, by our own skinnier standards, so generous in build they sometimes seem to overflow. In view of the poverty of their native, overcrowded islands, this reflects well upon their priorities; whatever else they go short of, it doesn't seem to be nourishment.

4

West Indian tenants tend to have their failings like everyone else. One is to be as careless and untidy outside their own family circle as they are clean within it. Stairs, landings, shared lavatories, yards, front steps, are often filthy; windows are unwashed and cracked; unemptied dustbins stink, children pee in the gardens, and it's the old story—everyone's property is no one's responsibility. Amongst white neighbours feelings of resentment breed as copiously as flies among the garbage, and those feelings nourish and sustain colour prejudice. "Filthy, those blacks." If the offenders were natives, it would be "Filthy, those Joneses."

Other Caribbean domestic habits and customs collide with our own. Most West Indians—especially Jamaicans, it seems, for Barbadians tend to be more circumspect—like loud music, noise in general, conviviality, visiting one another, keeping late hours on weekends, dancing and jiving, eating savoury stews and things like yams and cho-cho, frying fish in coconut oil, drinking rum if they can afford it, and generally having a high old time. Most English prefer to keep themselves to themselves and guard their privacy. Ours is a land of the wall, the high fence, the privet hedge—all descendants of the moated grange. No other country has such an elaborate network of laws to stop people treading on one another's toes; dogs have only to bark, cocks to crow, cats miaow, radios blare, youngsters jive, floors shake, aircraft buzz, motorcycles roar beyond a certain level of decibels, for injunctions to fly about like autumn leaves.

There've been many white complaints. "They made life hell for me," said a fellow tenant, a single woman, "knocking on my door at all hours; then they killed one of my cats by throwing lighted cigarettes at it." Others are afraid to go out at night because, they say, the coloured people carry knives. In Willesden a liaison officer, himself a Jamaican, appointed to the Town Hall to alleviate—or, better still, forestall—friction between white and coloured maintains a sort of fire brigade consisting of a mixed voluntary panel of citizens prepared to hurry, in pairs—one white, one coloured—to the scene of incipient friction and sort the trouble out. Noisy weekend parties and stinking garbage are the commonest causes of complaint.

Even quite innocuous Caribbean habits sometimes jar upon the natives. "There's a man who lies in bed every weekend," a Brixtonian complained, "with his feet out of the window—funny, isn't it?" Another said, "I can't get used to the way they keep their hats on indoors."

This is no new complaint against immigrants. Huguenot clergy were accustomed, unlike English Protestants, to wear headgear in church. Visitors to French churches in London emerged badly shaken. "A hat upon the head of a preacher in his sermons!" exclaimed, ironically, an observer well over two hundred years ago. "Bless us! It shocks the eyes, disturbs the mind, splits the heart!"

5. How to Buy Houses and Get Tenants Out

Noisy parties, dirty yards, outlandish cooking smells, hugger-muggering together, feet jutting out and hats clamped on—these and other personal habits are symptoms of strangeness, of being foreign; but the really significant source of friction lies deeper—competition. The more successful your competitor, the more you look around for someone or something to blame. If, into the bargain, he's an outsider, an intruder, then your xenophobia and your colour prejudice fuse. So wherever there's competition between immigrant and native, there's your tender spot, your home-based apartheid, your "Go home, nigger," and "Keep Britain white."

At the moment—this could change—it's the roof that matters most. Say you've been five years on the Council's housing list and had two more babies since your name went down; you're cramped and inconvenienced and frustrated, and now to cap it all an Indian or a *schwarz* (a Negro) has bought your lodging house. An immigrant who's been half as long in the country as your name's been on the housing list.

Now the whole street's going black; all sorts of queer foods

you've never heard of appear in the shops; fat, thrusting coloured women jostle you in the supermarket and elbow you
away from the stalls; they jump the bus queues, they stand
and gossip in loud voices in doorways, they think they own
the place; people say the men smoke reefers and live off girls.
White tenants have only to hear that a coloured man is after
the house to go around to the Town Hall and ask for help in
finding someplace else. "Why not wait and see what happens?" asks the housing officer. The white tenants shake anxious heads. "We've heard. Now it's going to happen to *us*."

There is, of course, no law to say that only immigrants can
buy houses; the first question anyone feels inclined to ask is,
if English people don't like coloured landlords, why don't
they save, borrow, and buy?

Most people of the English urban working class think in
terms of rent, not ownership; increasingly they tend to feel
the Council owes them a house; and of course, Council rents
are heavily subsidized. To buy through a building society
costs a lot more, and subletting is regarded as a separate occupation. Owning and subletting what are known as "houses
in multiple occupation" isn't part of our natural habit. And
then we lack the strong incentive of the immigrants.

Their saving often takes ingenious forms. Some West Indians practice a traditional system known in Jamaica as part-
nership and as *sou-sou* in Trinidad. A group of people club
together to contribute a fixed sum every week for a fixed
period. Let's say it's twenty people, three pounds a week
each, and six months. Each member takes his turn to draw
out a "hand." His full share comes to seventy-five pounds. He
draws this out according to his need; this week I've got the
chance to buy a house and want the cash immediately for the
deposit, so we all agree I take my whole hand now. Next

week you buy a double bed and take a part hand of fifteen pounds; the week after, it's someone else's turn. It's a sort of Christmas club, without the Christmas and more flexible; and it's helped many a West Indian landlord to get his start.

2

Few indeed are the immigrants who can track a path through the legal thickets of our housing, rent, and mortgage laws. There's a whole fringe world of shady agents and lawyers scouting like hyenas around the herds to pounce on laggards, and they're by no means all snow-white—this isn't a colour situation, it's a social one. Many of the dodges they get up to are too involved for any but aspiring Rachmans to grasp. Others are plain enough. A property agent asks an exorbitant price for one of the formerly unsalable, now sought-after, Victorian mansions on his books; the immigrant hasn't got the money; obligingly, the agent gives him an introduction to a mortgage company he thinks might listen sympathet- ically. As the agent owns the mortgage company, sympathy's forthcoming—at interest rates of anything up to 30 percent.

A down payment, an agreement, and there's another col- oured landlord—with commitments to pay enormous future sums. Even the agreement may be fiddled; I heard of a West Indian who'd been assured that, to be valid for three years or over, every legal agreement needed a stamp worth £150; he paid over the sum, only to learn, too late, that the stamp was faked and the agreement not worth a sheet of yesterday's newspaper.

If the landlord is to keep up his monthly payments, he must cram his house to the ridge beams with tenants and make them pay through the nose. He's got (in American parlance) a bear by the tail. Provided that he keeps his grip, it can be a very profitable bear indeed. Here's a typical example, by no means an extreme case. In a three-story house built for one family, with two dark basement rooms, six ordinary rooms, and a couple of back-passage spaces shared as kitchens or let as "rooms" to single men, dwelt nine separate families or "units," comprising twenty-two individuals. (West Indian, Pakistani, and Irish; the landlord, a Jamaican.)

A single, filthy water closet; no bathroom; everything cracked, peeling, unpainted, down-at-heel; garbage and discarded household debris (old mattresses, a broken armchair, rusty cans, broken bottles, worn-out clothing) littering what had once been a back garden, where now hungry cats prowl; and rents of three pounds a room rolling in—thirty pounds weekly net, plus extras and perks. (Landlords often fiddle the meter so that the tenant's shilling doesn't buy a shilling's worth of gas, and pocket the difference.) Some of these houses are turned into dormitories for single men and the beds let twice over, day workers and night-shift men taking turns, and playing cards together to pass the time on weekends.

3

Few but Mr. Ben Parkin, Member of Parliament for North Paddington, paid much attention to the "de-statting" racket until Miss Keeler and her friends drew aside the curtain on so many facets of our national life. Yet in Paddington Town Hall there's a dossier on Rachman, with all the facts, written three years before the lid blew off. By now "de-statting" has been so well documented that almost anyone could list at least half a dozen ways by which landlords can get rid of tenants they're legally obliged to keep at low, controlled rents, in order to make way for unprotected tenants who'll pay them very much more.

There are the famous West Indian parties, raging all night outside the statutory tenants' rooms; pounding on doors, thumping floors, throwing stones at windows; garbage un-collected, stairs fouled, jostlings, threats, jeers; gas cut off, deliveries stopped, and even, in extreme cases, men sent around to strip off the roof. Sometimes just a misleading law-yer's letter will do. A young Irishwoman came in tears into a Citizen's Advice Bureau the other morning, in Notting Hill; she'd arrived the night before with two small children, ex-hausted, in the dark; a single low-voltage light bulb had left the secrets of the dwelling unrevealed; the coloured landlord had demanded a down payment on the spot of fifty pounds. She'd paid him all she had, thirty, and discovered in the light of day a dreadful hovel, bug-infested, damp and dirty, only one ring working on the communal cooker, the communal lavatory stuffed up. She couldn't stand it, her cash was gone, what could she do?

It's fortuitous, but disastrous, that the landlords are often coloured, and the statutory tenants who are driven out invar-iably white, and generally old. Fundamentally this isn't a colour situation at all; it's just happened to work out that way because of social changes. But if you're a white tenant hounded out of your flat by a landlord who's flouting the law, you're naturally bitter; and if the landlord is dusky, it's natu-

ral, again, to mix up his colour and the fact that he's an
immigrant with your legitimate grievance; and then another
racist is born.

Responsible West Indians and Asians deplore behaviour
by their less scrupulous brethren that brings their whole race
into disrepute. "I am proud for my colour," an Asian landlord told me, explaining that he charged fair rents and tried
to keep his house tidy and in good repair. But deploring
never stops anything. What's wrong is the basic, simple fact
we started with—not enough living space to go around. The
immigrants, of course, have made the housing shortage worse.
"Because of them," remarked a public health authority,
"we're stuck with our slums for a whole generation longer."

In the last analysis, immigrants are coming because we
need their labour. Having got here, they have to find someplace to live. Since housing isn't keeping pace, an extra million people coming in was bound to mean an extra-tight
squeeze. The squeeze came and it hurt. It's been the greatest
single source of discord between immigrant and host. It still
is, and will continue to be. Immigrants, if you come to think
of it, haven't really brought new problems with them, or not
many; they've highlighted and sharpened the problems we
had already, and still have.

4

"If *we* packed in like that, the authorities would be down on
us in no time. *We'd* be in court, but not the blacks, they
break the law and everyone turns a blind eye." Over the

years a structure of laws, rules, and regulations has been erected precisely to prevent people from "living like pigs" in overcrowded dwellings. Then how have the immigrants escaped them? What has gone wrong?

If a property is past salvaging, the local authority can serve a compulsory purchase order on the owner and pull it down. To serve such an order you must first know who the owner is. Absurd as it may seem, sometimes this appears to be impossible. A group of Pakistanis, say, have clubbed together to buy a joint house. Even if an individual owner can be unravelled, he must, by law, be rehoused. This means he jumps the waiting list and is rehoused ahead of local citizens whose needs are much greater—the Pakistani is probably a single man—and whose names have been down for years. Naturally, the citizens become enraged. Here, again, it's not really a colour situation, but it looks like one, and stokes up the colour prejudice that local authorities lean a long way backwards to avoid.

And what happens to all the lodgers who've been packed into the condemned house? Although the local authority doesn't have to rehouse them too, they won't just vanish into thin air; they'll merely move into other overcrowded houses and exacerbate the situation there. I came across a case in Stepney, an appalling slum; a compulsory purchase order had been served, and the Jewish landlord had given notice to his lodgers. There were seventeen, all Pakistanis, sleeping on the shift system, two to a bed. Where would they go? They themselves would have found nothing unusual in bedding down in the street, but that doesn't fit in with either our ideas or our climate. Someone would have to do something, but no one knew what. In the face of all this you can hardly blame health authorities from walking like cats on hot bricks.

5

If the property's not bad enough to be demolished, but is sound enough to be repaired, the local authority may serve an order on the landlord directing him to bring it up to certain standards. These limit the number of people to a room and deal with sanitation—the usual ration is eight people to a water closet—and also cooking, storage of food, and the like.

Most health authorities consider these standards in themselves inadequate. Two people are allowed per room, and that includes the living rooms and anything larger than a cubbyhole. And there are loopholes. Before inspecting a house the health authority must give the landlord twenty-four hours' notice. So tenant families are bundled out and cross the street to pay a short visit to a fellow immigrant. The inspector finds only the statutory number of lodgers, and as soon as he's out of sight back flock the other tenants. This rule the new Housing Act proposes to change.

"The basic trouble is," said a public health inspector, "that we're trying to apply English housing standards, drawn up to meet English needs and conform to English living patterns, to an immigrant community with different living patterns and a different need." Or—another way of putting it—to apply urban standards to people of a rural outlook and a way of life evolved in a different society.

Most immigrants have much larger families than we do; on average, probably at least twice as large. (In Jamaica the birthrate is forty-three per thousand compared with seventeen in Britain—two and a half times as large.) And many West Indians and Indians *like* what we consider overcrowding; to them it's simply living in a normal, human, and convivial way. "Their whole life is centred in the family," an observer said. "Their children don't get on their nerves as ours do if we're tightly packed. They like sharing things. The women share their cookers, pots and pans, storage cupboards, everything. *Our* wives wouldn't be on speaking terms in those conditions, but not the West Indians; to them it's congenial; they have a different outlook from ours." This outlook the Italians share. "Unique in my experience," said a public health inspector in Bedford, "they're quite prepared to use the same cookers and sinks at the same time without falling out."

In warm climates you don't shut yourself up inside four walls, light the fire, and close the door against draughts and strangers. You have the open-sided shed, the outdoor cooking fire, people coming and going; you observe an ancient, deep, universal tradition of hospitality. To refuse a stranger, let alone a relative, food and shelter is a heinous crime. Now the immigrants are in our houses, built to meet a different need and match another outlook; and yet they haven't left their own outlook, their own traditions, their own customs and beliefs, behind.

Here's the root of the trouble, and once again it's not basically a colour situation, it's a culture clash: two sets of norms, of patterns, of ideas meeting head on in the back streets of Paddington and Notting Hill, Balsall Heath and Handsworth, Lumb Lane and Chapeltown. Basically this situation has prevailed ever since a world of cultivators began to take to towns. Wessex peasants displaced by the enclosures;

Irish peasants driven forth by the potato famine; now West Indian and Asian peasants lured by pay and jobs; they come to cities, pack into slums, wander like babes in the wood through forests not just of brick and concrete but of different ideas. The adjustment's always painful and difficult. At least the Wessex and the Irish peasants *looked* the same, even if they weren't; you couldn't tell them from their hosts on the street. Now, with the newest peasants, you can.

6. Coconuts in Ladbroke Grove

NOT ALL landlords are sharks, not all tenants persecuted, all landings filthy, and all houses going downhill. Quite a number of immigrant landlords are improving their property, and more will do so. Birmingham has issued a pamphlet addressed in thirteen languages to owners of multiple-occupied dwellings that asks, "Is your house alive or dead?" and explains how the kiss of life can be administered, if necessary with loans of up to 85 percent. Only about 300 of their 5,000 immigrant-owned houses remain on the sick list. No doubt a similar story could be told elsewhere.

When immigrants start buying in a district, generally the value of property falls. (There are exceptions to this: in the case of very slummy houses the newcomers may create a fresh demand.) Partly the usual drop is due to sheer prejudice among the natives, partly to a fear that immigrants will introduce the values of the slums they're moving out of into districts hitherto considered "nice."

These fears are nearly always unfounded. It's precisely the immigrants' intention not to live like pigs, but like middle-class English people, that forms their main incentive to move. They want to adopt British standards, to be accepted, to become inconspicuous. A housing officer observed, "These coloured landlords don't *want* their houses to fall to bits. Still less do they want to be looked down on and criticized. They come here and say, 'We want to live like you.' Half the trouble is they don't know what to do. It's our job to help them find out."

And there's another obstacle. Many are impeded by a dream. For the Caribbean it's a well-found little bungalow on a sunlit hillside with banana trees and flamboyants all around, in a favoured part of Kingston or Nassau, Georgetown or Port-of-Spain. A warm sea, a shady tree, freedom and laughter, coconuts and yams, fellowship and sunshine.

"I miss the young coconut," said a sad Dominican girl nursing her baby in a back street off Ladbroke Grove. Yams, cho-cho, dayshin, sweet potatoes, breadfruit, pomegranates— London's barrows and little greengrocers' are piled with exotic eatables smelling of the home most West Indians want to return to, but never will. It costs about one thousand pounds to get a family of five or six—and few families are smaller— back to the Caribbean.

Meanwhile their intentions are closely linked to the housing situation. The better this is, the more reconciled do they become to settling down in Britain for good. It is worst in London, and here, according to a sample poll in 1961, over half the West Indians hoped to go home. On the other hand, in Nottingham, where pressure is much lighter, only one in ten was bent on repatriation, and seven out of ten had resolved to settle for good.

Leeds ranked next to Nottingham in satisfaction rating, with one in five wanting to go home and two thirds to settle. (Leeds has one of the best housing records in the country: over 3,000 families housed annually, half in flats, the city

owning 50,000 dwellings, and only 2 percent of immigrants.)
The Irish and the Cypriots were the least desirous of returning to their homeland, Pakistanis most so. But in Leeds even
the Pakistanis were evenly divided between stayers and goers.

The longer people stay, the more their dream evaporates.
Some *do* leave, and then come back; they've become used to a
different way of life and find the old way has lost its appeal. I
met a Sikh who'd been in Britain ten years, saved, bought a
house, sold it at a profit, and gone back to his village in the
Punjab; but it wasn't the same. "People want to know everything you do. And then there're no amenities. I took a cooker
to my daughter; with the freight, it cost me a hundred pounds.
It's still in the crate, waiting for electricity. When you're used
to cookers, you don't like going back to paraffin stoves."

So, back in Britain with his wife and family, he's bought
another house, and a smart new Cortina stood outside the
door. Drizzle, cold, smog? "Inside we're warm and comfortable. The children get a good education and good jobs,
whereas in India—millions unemployed."

Coloured immigrants are beginning to follow the pattern
set by their predecessors. They start in slums, get a foothold,
work and save, and finally stratify and disperse. In Leeds's
Chapeltown you can see the process enshrined in bricks and
mortar: first a handsome synagogue—several others have followed their congregations north to Moortown and elsewhere;
up the road, a Polish club; almost opposite, the Sikhs have
recently bought a disused chapel and converted it into a
temple.

In London a trickle of West Indians and Indians has be-
gun to move towards areas like Finsbury, Tottenham, and
Harrow. Hampstead's population is already over 25 percent
immigrant, but of these immigrants only one in six is col-

oured—just under 5 percent of the total. Among London's boroughs Paddington and Kensington have the highest proportion of coloured folk.

How high? No one can be sure. Even the census figures aren't accurate. A good many West Indians dodged the census of 1961 because they feared prosecutions for overcrowding should their real numbers have been revealed. Since 1961 thousands more have come. And those born here do not, of course, count as immigrants. The Reverend Clifford Hill, who made a study of the West Indians, estimated that the true figure for Caribbeans in London was twice as large as that arrived at in the census—150,000 instead of 70,000. In Paddington, whatever the official figure, the knowledgeable estimate is that at least one resident in ten is coloured. Between 1951 and 1961 the number of immigrants in the county of London as a whole rose, officially, by 52 percent, with Paddington, Kensington, and Stoke Newington, in that order, in the lead.

Caribbeans are still the most numerous, but Indians and Pakistanis are coming in more rapidly. Indians save more quickly; a few—exceptions, naturally—are well on the way to becoming property tycoons. In the Midlands, I encountered a Bengali who, ten years ago, had started work in a factory, unskilled, at four pounds a week. He sent for his wife, she went to work as well, and their joint income rose to eight pounds; they saved, borrowed, and bought their first house. Now he runs a company that owns forty houses, and is negotiating for another twenty-five. He lives in style, sits on local committees, and takes a hand in civic affairs.

Elsewhere a more tempestuous character—a lapsed Sikh— worked up to seven houses, which he rents on double shifts to Pakistanis; each bed brings in two pounds a week and he clears about £250 a week from his property. Or did. "He doesn't know how to spend the money," a Pakistani acquaintance said with some contempt. "He gambles and drinks. One night he gambled away two of his houses"—like an eighteenth-century English milord dicing at White's for horses, coaches, and finally the family estate.

2

Because most lack skills, nearly all coloured immigrants enter our society at the bottom of the status scale. They fill the position that used to belong to Irish labourers. Eight West Indians out of ten are classified as unskilled or semi-skilled, and only 2 percent as "professional and managerial," compared with 25 percent of Indian immigrants. Many Caribbeans say they're downgraded here into the lowest-paid and dirtiest jobs the natives disdain. "We get what the Englishman doesn't want—the room he won't live in, the job he won't take, and the woman he throws out." Often there's an undertone of self-pity among the Caribbeans. They cry colour bar; but lack of skill and training plus a nonindustrial, peasant background may often be more telling reasons for their disabilities.

There's a considerable gap between British and Caribbean notions of what is skilled and what isn't. In a sample of Dominicans working here one third of those who classified themselves as skilled had to be rejected. "A man," the sampler commented, "would claim to be a painter or a mechanic simply because, in some remote past, he had held a brush or even watched someone else handling these implements." No doubt some immigrants are working here with wasted skills, but seldom the kind of skill that industry most needs; demand is too keen to let much go to waste.

And it's still the natives who perform most of the less well-rewarded and more strenuous tasks. Farm work ranks among the lower paid jobs, as well as one of the most exacting, and there are virtually no coloured farm workers. There are coloured workers on the building sites, but on the whole, most employers needing men for strenuous tasks prefer the Irish. And a sample taken in London in 1960 showed that one third of all West Indian men had reached a skilled category and were spread over fifty different occupations.

What, of course, has happened is that colour has been mixed up with class. You get the rotten jobs; you don't get promotion; people are morose in the canteen. It's all because you're coloured. Try to convince a Jamaican that it's not his colour, it's because he's unskilled, he's not suitable, and that's the nature of the British workingman, and he'll never believe you. Sometimes he'll be right, but not nearly so often as he thinks.

"I keep on trying to ram it home to them that it's all happened to me." This was from the son of a Nottingham-shire coal miner. "When I was a boy, we were a race apart. The local squire didn't know we existed. I couldn't have walked up to his front door; I couldn't even go to the front door of the solicitor. It was round at the back and touch your cap. I was white enough, even if my father wasn't when he came off shift. It's not colour, it's class—their fight's the same as ours. But they won't see it.

"The other day I went to see an old Welshwoman who'd been in lodgings in a house in Paddington bought by a coloured man. She'd moved into an institution rather than stay on with a coloured landlord. 'I came here sixty years ago from Glamorgan,' she said in her Welsh voice. 'Been Labour all my life, a good trade unionist, too,' and then she poured out her troubles. She hadn't even seen the landlord—'black as anthracite, they say, coming in and taking our houses and driving us out . . .' Then I went to see the landlord; he *was* black as anthracite; he asked me in. 'I came here thirty years ago from Glamorgan,' he said in a Welsh voice. 'Been Labour all my life, a good trade unionist, too . . .' He'd been born in Cardiff."

"Riddled with tensions" was the verdict on Paddington by one of its social workers. And for the usual cause. Coloured immigrants are buying up every dwelling they can afford, and that means fag ends of leaseholds and houses full of statutory tenants, mostly elderly. "Immigrants just don't understand old ladies living alone. With them it never happens. They ask, why don't these old folk join their families or buy places of their own? And then the coloured landlords need the higher rents to keep up their payments, so they resort to petty persecution. Coloured young men bullying white old ladies—resentment again."

There's only one answer: more dwellings. Where? The borough owns very little land and prices are astronomical. Nine families have been wiped off the housing list in four years. Ludicrous, if it weren't tragic.

Virtually no compulsory purchase orders have been made, though many houses richly deserve them. (Those with willow-pattern lavatory pans are generally considered to be ripe for demolition.) Where would the occupants go? For a London County Council house there's a waiting list of 50,000 families, with about 1,000 coming off the list every year. "The old and elderly are buttoned up in the borough—trapped. So they've just got to put up with persecution and hang on."

What about hostels for the immigrants; at any rate, the single men? Most social workers are against these. They smack of segregation, for one thing; for another, they discriminate. Immigrants are entitled to the same treatment as our own people, no worse, but no better. Why (ask social workers) should immigrants get preference over children in need of care and protection, over the handicapped, delinquents, ex-prisoners wanting aftercare? All are in the same boat. Probation and children's officers grow almost desperate with frustration, lacking children's homes, centres for aftercare, clubs, clinics. The immigrants are mostly young and healthy men. Should they get priority over, say, handicapped children? And few immigrants complain openly; they don't want to call attention to themselves. "I'd rather put up with injustice than be martyred for it," one of them said.

They arrive with the wish to be accepted by the host society. Is their wish being gratified? You see and hear two contradictory tendencies. At work and in the schools there's pretty fair integration, considering; little overt trouble, anyway. But social intermingling? In the pubs, any evening, you can see, as plain as ink and whitewash, sheep and goats. The penlike structure of the English pub has made this separation easy to achieve. (In a Continental café this would not be so.) Black in one bar, white in the other, a wooden partition in between. A strange sight in an English pub.

This, the publicans say, is not their doing, it's the customers'. Not a word said, these divide by mutual agreement— like W. S. Gilbert's lay of the two Englishmen wrecked on a desert island and cut off from all communication with each other because they'd not been introduced.

And somehow thus they settled without a word of mouth,
That Gray should take the northern half while Somers took
   the south.

In the white pen not a single black face intruded; on the
black side a couple of palefaces drifted in. One had a Penguin
Special protruding from a pocket, a Committee for Nuclear
Disarmament badge, and an ingratiating smile. "An intellectual trying to soft-soap his way in," my companion said
with some acidity. This companion was a tough, Paddington-
Irish, ex-Guards N.C.O. who was trying, with scant success, to
organize youth clubs. The West Indians talked melodiously
among themselves, paid the paleface no attention, and kept
their hats clamped firmly on. The other native, looking like a
dour and well-dressed bank manager, sat in glum silence gaz-
ing at his beer, quaffed it, and walked out. "The secretary of
a local Communist branch." No proselytizer, he. In the white
pen two or three customers struck up one of those maudlin,
self-conscious Irish songs. Outside, the dark, wet streets were
empty, litter-strewn, and sad. Kingston, Jamaica, and Paddington, London, lie worlds apart.

But down in dirty basements under peeling houses are
whiffs of Kingston, Nassau, Port-of-Spain. You squeeze past a
smelly lavatory and through a paintless door guarded by
bouncers into the low-ceilinged, tightly sealed-off place as
dark and private as a womb. The centre is bare for dancing,
there's a bench all around, a small soft-drink bar. (No license.)

A radio blares out pop music at full blast. The men wear
hats at saucy angles, the women stiletto heels and tight cot-
tons and high, de-kinked hairdos. There's a thick fog of cigarette smoke with a *ganja* undertone. On Saturdays jiving and
twisting don't get under way before midnight, and go on till
winter dawn. Tucked away out of the sight of cold, censori-

ous eyes, here's a corner of a foreign field that is temporarily, if not forever, Caribbean: warmth, companionship, music, rhythm, love, and laughter—a party, spontaneity and song.

Down the road, a coffee bar. Here the long-haired, loutish, tightly trousered palefaced customers look glum and hollow-minded, like young dogs to whom the snarl's more natural than the wag; the girls are sloppy, would-be sexy, predictable as a pop disc. For both the porpoise just behind them, labelled *ennui,* is always treading on their tails. Youth clubs they consider corny, physical exercise repellent, and agrophobia haunts the great outdoors. Here the healthy influence of Prince Philip is minimal. "A barrier it's very hard to penetrate," the would-be youth club organizer said.

He took me, however, to a coffee bar whose owner has turned it into an informal sort of teenage club and tried to get a bit of life into it, a hint of sophistication, even a *soupçon* of *esprit de corps:* bright curtains, a star-spangled ceiling, clean crockery, contemporary paintings on the walls. A radio blares, but there's no dancing—he can't get a license (technicalities to do with fire), and every time his teenagers start to twitch or tap their feet they break the law. There have been prosecutions. But they come in droves, drink coffee, smoke and talk, even laugh now and then.

White faces here, 100 percent. Colour bar? The adults shook their heads. "Not on our part. The coloured kids just don't come. They wouldn't be welcome. To start with, a few came in threes and fours, and they had only one idea, pick up girls. There wasn't a fight, but there could have been. It's the wrong age. No one's going to stand by and see another fellow take his girl. And if it's a coloured boy, in no time you can have a race riot on your hands."

It's the wrong age. Wherever you go, the same story. In

primary schools, no trouble; children very soon cease to notice, if they ever start to do so, colour of skin. Then come adolescence, spots, sex, and indoctrination by adults; with those, suspicion and prejudice. A social progression.

Is sex the taproot of prejudice? Probably. The ultimate test of all good intentions in regard to integration is the corny old question, would you like your daughter to marry a Negro? Or, no less, would you allow your daughter to marry a white? Few honest fathers, British or coloured, would return to this question a genuine, unhedged "Yes." Most Asian fathers react as if stung by a snake.

It's not even a question of colour. "If my daughter married out of the faith, I'd disown her for good," a Jew in Leeds told Dr. Ernest Krausz. "We just don't mix—the feeling isn't there," said another. "You're born like an animal into a certain breed."

Slowly but, no doubt, surely, intermarriage grows; there's a gradual blurring of the perimeters of each community. The strongest obstacle appears, at present, to be male jealousy. Fathers guard their daughters and the young male, like the robin and the hippopotamus, keeps rivals off his territory.

7. The Silent Italian

FOR EIGHT WEEKS a Bedford primary school boy sat at his desk and moved like an automaton to playground, canteen, and cloakroom without speaking a single word. His teachers coaxed, cajoled, ignored, reasoned, tried everything to break through a barrier as intangible as it was impenetrable. The child might have been a Martian; they just couldn't get through.

He was an Italian. His parents proved no help at all. The father was out all day, and the mother, enraged at being summoned from work, ejected a stream of dialect—like one of those sea squids pumping out an inky fluid lethal to its foes —which no one, not even older Italian pupils, could understand. Italian dialects vary so widely as sometimes to baffle even fellow countrymen from the next valley. But all are mixed in Bedford schools.

In Islington a Cypriot boy remained speechless for a whole term. And in Nottingham a German-Lithuanian boy, who spoke both those languages but no English, sat in frozen silence for over a month.

After eight weeks the Bedford headmaster was summoned

so excitedly to a classroom that he thought a fire had broken out. The silent Italian child's lips were moving. Very softly he was muttering, "One, two, three . . ." It was an emotional moment for everyone. After that the boy quickly returned to normal. So did the Cypriot, and in Nottingham the teacher managed to get across the notion that the boy should draw what he'd had for dinner. She kept on making guesses—she knew a little German—until she hit upon a cabbage and he nodded; contact between them was established, and his mind began to thaw.

This prolonged total silence seems to be a symptom of acute mental shock. The child is being asked to live simultaneously in two unconnected worlds. His half-formed mind is tugged like a cord stretched between two opposing forces. To avoid snapping, the conscious mind sensibly withdraws. Since the world around him makes no sense at all, the child locks himself into a fortress, hoists the drawbridge, and gives up trying. This is a situation no teacher has previously met with in British schools.

We are mistaken always to be thinking of immigrants in terms of colour. The real barrier is not colour, or even language, though that is much more formidable: it's a barrier of outlook, culture, values, way of life. Language is a part of it, but not all.

West Indians share the English tongue and, more or less, English culture. This the Caribbeans have indeed modified and perhaps arrested, since it was transplanted three centuries ago and remains in the main pre-industrial; but in the old British colonies they've had no other culture to confuse or rival it. Slavery destroyed the one they brought with them from Africa, and they adopted ours with our language. British teachers soon discovered that to educate West Indian children confronted them with very minor problems compared with those presented by our fellow Europeans such as Italians and Cypriots.

2

Italians started to arrive in Bedford in 1952, recruited by the Ministry of Labour. Soon numbers swelled until there are now between 6,000 and 7,000, and about 1,000 children in the schools out of a total roll of 8,600. (Although Bedford is only one of several nuclei of Italians, it is the most concentrated; there is a nest of market gardeners at Hoddesdon in Hertfordshire, and there are many Italians in the Midlands, and much older colonies in Clerkenwell and Soho; altogether, probably around 60,000 have settled in the country as a whole.)

Most Bedford schools have some Italians, but four carry the biggest load. In three of these less than half the children are British; in one nursery school less than one third. Among the children at a junior school I visitied, thirteen tongues can be heard. (Bedford schools in general have children of thirty different nationalities.) The immigrant proportion in this school has been up to two thirds, and now stands at just about half, of whom the great majority are Italian (Indians next).

At first they came in driblets, at all ages and all stages of the school year, as ignorant of the language as so many stuffed owls. Like the Caribbeans, they came from peasant families.

Uprooted from the poorest parts of southern Italy, including Sicily, they had lived in extreme poverty, without a clue to any of the material furnishings we take for granted. They had never used a water closet, a knife and fork, a handkerchief, let alone a blackboard, a book, a traffic crossing, stairway, or electric light. They had run wild on barren hillsides herding goats, without shoes.

"Their background was so different," remarked the headmaster, "it was another world, another outlook, a completely different pattern of ideas. Life had made very few demands. Punctuality meant nothing. Time flowed on. They had no idea of discipline, their parents had no ambitions as we understand the word. They'd never even seen a book. They'd come and gone as they liked and sat in the sun. They understood nothing, and our sort of life was totally strange."

And here they were, deposited by mothers on their way to work on the doorsteps of teachers, cut off from all communication by the language barrier. If the teachers wanted to explain how to open a cupboard door or hold a pencil, they had to do it in mime. They had to conduct "lavatory drill." No special staff came in to help them at the start, and none of the teachers then spoke Italian.

Total chaos must, at times, have reigned; the miracle is that it didn't last. Rising to the occasion, improvising, doing our best with our backs to the wall—these are traditional British virtues, kept, as a rule, in cold storage, ready for the next war. Now these teachers dug them out and dusted them off. This was a crisis; by and large, the teachers met it with ingenuity, spirit, and almost unbelievable patience. "I've never been so proud of my colleagues," said an education officer in a town hall. Teachers get a lot of knocks, but on this occasion a purse of ha'pence seems justified.

3

"We start," said the Bedford headmaster, "with a simple proposition, that each child is not a problem but an individual—an individual we welcome and want. Not an outsider. We try to make each child feel that we are interested in everything about him—his mind, his body, his teeth, his hair, the way he uses the lavatory. It's a question of social training. That comes first. Making every one of them feel he's part of the community. I won't allow any derogatory words to be used here by the English children—nigs, wops, Itie, that sort of thing. The only exception was a child called Zona. I didn't mind the nickname Ariz."

Children will pick up a language very quickly; the social habits, the outlook, of a strange community take much longer, especially when you have the children only six or seven hours a day for five days a week. For the rest of the time they're back in their own tight, warm, transplanted family, speaking and hearing nothing but their native tongue, eating their own kind of food, living their own kind of life. They're pitched to and fro between the two worlds like a shuttle, and no wonder some of them express their bewilderment by what is now called antisocial behaviour but used to have blunter names. Sometimes they scream and fight and bite and kick and rush out of school with a distracted teacher in hot pursuit. Children's fighting habits, it seems, vary by races and nations: the English punch (male) and slap (female); Caribbeans and Italians kick (male) and bite (female); the Irish spit.

"That's something the English children won't tolerate," a teacher said. "In some schools the Irish are the toughest problem of the lot."

"We base our teaching methods," the Bedford headmaster continued, "on real life situations, not on books and blackboards. The children learn as they go along, by doing things. The language follows, it's part of what they're doing. We don't teach it, they find it out for themselves.

"For instance, most of the Italians are pretty good with their fingers: at practical activities, modelling, making things. We started basketwork—something to give them a feeling of accomplishment, of pleasure, quick joy; and a meaningful basis for the language. They learned the words for cane, fibre, plait, weave, and so forth. The language then becomes a part of living, not a thing apart. The living situation is what matters; the language is like foliage round the trunk of a tree."

4

The snag to all this is that teachers can't be doing more than two or three things at one time. They can't simultaneously be initiating Giuseppe into the mysteries of a water closet, showing John how to add and subtract, repeating to Clara the English for chimney, and helping Marilyn to put the rivers into a map of the United States. And John and Marilyn are faced with the eleven plus, or whatever system has replaced it. The extra demands made on teachers already at full stretch must lead inevitably to a dilution of effort, a slowing down. Is this fair to British children? Must standards fall?

English parents are understandably worried. There have been open protests in some places. However well teachers may have coped, however great their extra effort, *some* adverse effect there must have been.

"Standards did fall at first," this headmaster agreed. "But we managed to keep the 'A' stream going and our percentage of eleven-plus successes didn't drop. Against whatever academic loss there was for the English children, you've got to set the gain in social experience. They've learned a lot—not just a few words of Italian but the value of tolerance, of helping others, that foreigners aren't devils with horns or figures of fun, but human beings. Isn't that a net gain?"

In the long run it is the English custom, habit, way of life, that must set the pattern. It's the immigrants who will be absorbed. This Italian parents resent, even while they know it to be inevitable. Even if they themselves return one day to Italy, most of the children will stay behind. But probably few parents *will* return.

Meanwhile they feel their children being sucked away, adopting values they don't understand and often disapprove of—the freedom of the young, for instance, their independence and their sexual laxity. These Italians have a strong family cohesion. Frugal, hard-working, sober citizens—their crime record is considerably lower than the natives'—they go home at night, draw the curtains, and stick together. Now their teenage children are going off to movies and cafés and dance halls, throwing away money on pop records and even motor bikes.

Unlike the Poles, these British Italians have made few attempts to keep up their Italianness by means of newspapers, films, books, clubs, and so on. Roman Catholic missions with a small establishment of priests and nuns are probably the chief communal link. Some think that even this is weakening.

The greatest visible impact they seem to have made on English life—and that isn't strong—is in regard to food. Delicatessen shops stocking all sorts of appetizing Italian eatables and wines are common, but most of the customers seem to be other Italians or fellow immigrants. (There are reckoned to be over thirty-six different minorities in Bedford, including some 350 Yugoslavs, 500 Poles, and rather more Ukrainians.) Now even supermarkets have taken up foreign foods. In one, in Bedford's bustling, replanned new centre, you can buy Italian mortadella, Vienna lederhase, pistachio Parisier, knackwurst, debricina, kassler, lachsschinken, Spanish chorizos, kabanosi, Hungarian gulyás, Westphalian chasseurs, zebrezeina, Czech braun, chicken cacciatori, or Liptauer cheese (spellings, courtesy of the market manager), while the bus waits outside to take you to your semi-detached on the new housing estate and your appointment with the TV. But most Bedfordians stick to packaged chops, New Zealand cheddar, and frozen peas.

"I don't remember the Italian for 'window' or 'ceiling'; every day I'm forgetting more and more!" Irena of *The Three Sisters* cried in despair. In Bedford, Italian children are forgetting the Italian for everything so quickly that parents can no longer communicate with their own offspring. So a teacher has been sent from Italy to teach Italian to Italian children in Bedford schools.

5

Well after the first, unprepared-for wave of immigrant children had swept into the schools and chaos was beginning to subside, the slowly grinding wheels of authority began to churn out solutions. These vary from place to place.

The most usual is to set up special classes for non-English-speakers where they can be taught all subjects except those involving group activities—dancing, singing, physical training, art, and so on—and their English concentrated on until they understand enough to be drafted into the appropriate normal class. There's been a lively demand for teachers with a knowledge of Urdu, Gujarati, Punjabi, Hindi, and other Asian tongues.

At first many British teachers resisted the idea of special classes on the grounds that these were a concession to the principle of segregation. Almost to a man and woman teachers are ardent integrationists. This is an issue of emotional and religious belief on which humanists feel just as strongly—sometimes even more so—as Christians do. The least whiff of segregation reeks of sulphur and makes hairs bristle, hackles rise. Teachers would resign in droves rather than countenance that.

"You can't tell which is which," proudly said a Bedford headmaster as we watched a class of pupils with coffee skins, chocolate skins, olive skins, and white in the physical training period. "We're turning them all British." At first he had refused to introduce special classes, preferring to throw his non-English children in at the deep end and hold them up individually until they could swim. But where the proportion of immigrants tops a certain level—possibly around 25 or 30 percent—most teachers come around to "reception classes," mainly because they're now convinced that children learn best from instructors with a special knowledge of the art of teaching English to the non-English-speaking child. They can dodge the danger of apartheid by mixing up the children on every other possible occasion in the school. (It is the lack of mixing after school that troubles them.) As soon as the child has mastered sufficient English, he takes his place in the mainstream of academic life.

Birmingham has engaged itinerant teachers to move from school to school, giving special English instruction to the non-English-speakers, numbering at least 1,000. Well over 10,000 immigrant children now attend the city's schools—just about 6 percent overall, though one quarter of the schools have over 10 percent—and the number is rising smartly, partly because more immigrants are continually arriving, partly because their birthrate is much higher than ours.

An estimate that the number of nonnative children due to enter one particular secondary school, whose "catchment area" holds a substantial settlement of immigrants, will rise from four at present to over four hundred in ten years' time suggests that in years ahead the task of integration will grow tougher, not easier. Infants will hatch into adolescents and more and more children of immigrants roll off the assembly lines. Most of the immigrants are young and in the early stages of producing their ample broods; birth control among the majority is probably unheard of, and very often unwanted. Our social services are directed towards encouraging, not limiting, fecundity.

In Leeds there is a nursery school where out of three hundred tots only about seventy are British—some 23 percent. Others include Caribbeans, Indians, Pakistanis, Latvians, Poles, Ukrainians, Irish, Austrians, Czechs, Yugoslavs, Jews, Greeks, Chinese, and Maltese. Here an Englishwoman who speaks Hindi instructs a batch of non-English-speakers in all subjects until they can take their places in ordinary classes; after that the children teach their parents English.

Despite the swamping of the British the headmistress has not had one parental complaint. An active parents' association meets fortnightly, and every month there's a concert, or the children dance in their national costumes, which they're encouraged to wear. (The Caribbean national costume? "They like gay ribbons in their hats.") This attempt to integrate the parents meets with most success among West Indians; a few English parents come, but fewer Irish and Indians, and no Pakistanis or Chinese.

6

It's in secondary schools that the problem is most acute. At this age children don't pick up languages so quickly, and feel isolated and despondent; the work is such that if they can't follow they are lost, and the danger is greater that they'll hold back native pupils. So at three centres, one each in Islington, Camberwell, and Battersea, the London County Council has engaged a special staff to teach non-English-speakers, gathered in from a number of surrounding secondary schools, for one period every day. They also run special classes in those boroughs—Islington, St. Pancras, and Step-ney—where the immigrant proportion is particularly high.

Middlesex is launching an ambitious plan to take on fifty extra teachers, at a cost of over £50,000 a year, to instruct non-English-speakers, who cluster especially in Southall, Wil-lesden, and Hornsey. Willesden alone has over 3,000 immi-grant children, and everywhere the number is rising pretty sharply, and will continue to rise.

Huddersfield channels all its non-English-speakers, of whatever age, into a single school, now about 50–50 immi-grant and native, where specialist teachers enable them to master English relatively quickly, and then pass on into the normal classes. Recently a "language laboratory" has been installed to speed up the process of learning.

Nottingham, on the other hand, takes the view that special classes isolate the immigrants, who do better grafted onto the ordinary classes of the school. This has worked, by and large, satisfactorily, but that may be because hitherto the propor-tion of non-British has been low enough to enable the teach-ers to cope. This is changing. I visited a nursery school which was already one third immigrant, and the latest batch of new admissions mustered three coloured children to every English child.

No doubt there are pockets of resistance—Colin Jordan was a teacher—but nowhere in the schools have I myself encoun-tered any disagreement as to *whether* integration was the aim; the only question under discussion was how best it could be achieved.

8. Bubble and Squeak

ISLINGTON is full of Greek Cypriots. Some were there before the war, but most came during the Eoka troubles; now there are probably between 6,000 and 7,000, largely café owners and tailors. Very few spoke any English when they came, especially the women. And they want to stay Greek; they want their children to stay Greek, too, and they resent steps towards integration. We, as hosts, are so apt to think of integration as the great and only good, and to regard anyone who doesn't ardently promote it as a secret apartheid addict, that it comes as a shock to realize how many immigrants reject it, often with passion. Like Poles and Jews, Cypriots want to fit in but not to be swallowed.

And, like Bedford's Italians, they come from peasant homes and pre-industrial conditions; to them life in a great modern city is as strange as life in the Yemen would be to confirmed Londoners. As for schools, the mothers tend to look on them as crèches; they dump their little ones on the steps of the nursery school on their way to work at eight o'clock and fetch them at six on their way home.

Nearly all the Cypriot women work, and that is why, in English opinion, they manage to save. An Islington woman on a bus complained, "Most English girls, if they've got small kids, don't work all day, not full shifts like this lot do. So the Greeks get more money, and then they come in and buy our houses." This they are doing, like the Indians and Caribbeans. A teacher commented, "They work harder and go without things. The children don't know what toys are."

The teachers at this nursery school have, at first, to explain everything by gestures: how to hold a pencil, how to hang up a coat, and (as usual) how to use the lavatory. "When they come, the Jamaican girls stand up and pee on the seats," a teacher explained. "And they're totally illiterate. This is bound to slow down the pace for the English children in the lower forms. So far we've managed to keep up the standards in the top forms, but it's been a struggle."

They have no extra staff except a seventy-year-old part-time teacher who comes three mornings a week to take a special English class. Six languages are native to her pupils at present: Greek, Turkish, Italian, Hindi, and two Nigerian tongues. Out of last term's entry of twenty-nine children eleven had no English at all. There are, by now, 2,700 Cypriot children in London County Council schools. Every year the number rises, as it will continue to do.

This particular nursery school has been open for ten years. For the first three years it had three non-English pupils. By 1960 this has risen to ten. Now there are 163, which represents 55 percent of the roll. The bulk are Cypriots, and there are fourteen other nationalities, including (in this order) Irish, West Indian, Indian, Nigerian, Latvian, Czech, Polish, Spanish, Mauritian, and Burmese. Last term's entry had nine English children out of thirty-five. As we watched a class catapulting out of its classroom for the morning break

("They're uninhibited," their teacher drily remarked), the head commented, "There isn't an English child in sight."

For the teacher it's a challenge, and also a severe strain. "Each child needs individual attention and a lot of time and understanding; they're bewildered, and that can make them difficult; we've got a maladjusted Jamaican who goes berserk sometimes and screams and spits and bites and runs out into the street and takes up endless time. Most classes have forty children, and we just can't give them the individual attention they need. The major problem of organization is finding something constructive for the rest to do while the one on whom you're concentrating gets his individual care."

Nowadays many of our young teachers are going to the so-called underdeveloped countries for Voluntary Service Overseas among the primitives. Meanwhile a lot of primitives from underdeveloped countries are coming here. It's less glamorous to teach Nigerians in Stoke Newington than in Ibadan, Pakistanis in Southall than in Chittagong, but it's probably even more useful. As well as VSO we badly need a VSH—H for Home—A British Peace Corps for London's boroughs and the back streets of Birmingham.[1]

2

Everyone who traffics with children agrees that dislike of other groups of humans is not inborn. Small children just

[1] I have since learned than an organization of this nature does exist: Community Service Volunteers (15 Trinity Square, London E.C.3), whose members, mostly young people between school and college ages, are performing a variety of public-spirited and often challenging tasks (such as helping to care for delinquents and mental deficients), including the teaching of immigrant children in London and Birmingham.

don't notice whether an individual is black or white, speaks Greek or Gujarati. Later prejudice is born.

Partly, no doubt, this is a result of growing experience; as the child's mind develops, he learns the habit of transferring to some other creature responsibility for his own frustrations and shortcomings; the nignogs and the wops atone for the failures of Mike and Reggie. Partly the growing child becomes his parents' echo. Few of us are original thinkers in our early teens, and so we just regurgitate the views of adults all around us, thus perpetuating the beliefs, outlooks, and prejudices of our own kind. Indeed, that is how culture is transmitted. Culture's a mixed bag.

At a comprehensive school in Islington, with a roll of over 1,000 pupils, one quarter of them non-British, Mr. Taysir Kawwa, a young Lebanese sociologist, estimated that 85 percent of the boys and girls of all groups, immigrant and native alike, nourish feelings of prejudice against other groups. This has nothing to do with colour. The largest foreign group consists of Greek Cypriots. (Bubble and squeaks, in rhyming slang.) Out of the 777 questioned, only one child mentioned colour, and the British held Cypriots in less esteem than West Indians.

"They take our jobs"—one could hardly have a clearer example of regurgitation. "They come over here and take our houses and turn them into slums. Myself, I think they get jobs as easy as a finger snap, for us we are thousands out of work, they should give the white people first chance." (Regurgitation of the fear complex: there's very little unemployment now in Islington.) "I would like to get hold of every single one of them and put them on a plane and send them back where they come from."

Some remarks reflected sad experiences. "A black man

bought the house of my aunt; we was living there comfortable, but when we heard we just had to move out, this man really stunk terrible and he was on his own." Others reflected popular myths. "Sometimes they put chickens in the bathroom." Some just know their parents' minds without bothering about reasons. "I don't like Cypriots simply because I don't like them and because they take liberties."

A kindlier note was struck about West Indians. "I would like the black people to be treated as if they was English, but not the Greek Cypriots as they would try to get in to be a Member of Parliament in England." A few of the children took a more philosophic view. "Myself, I think that if you treat them horrible, call them all the black names, etc., they will call you all the milky names they can, so the best thing is if you take no notice of them, let them play the fool but they look little as hell." One went to the heart of the matter with engaging simplicity. "I like them if they are friendly. I do not like them if they are not friendly." Very few made close friends outside his own national or racial group. Each group, in fact, preferred itself to others.

As the children get to know each other and are influenced by their teachers, does prejudice evaporate? From the headmaster's window we watched West Indian, Cypriot, Indian, and English boys kicking a football about happily together, while the girls played tag, white and brown and olive. "You wouldn't have seen that a year ago," said the head.

On the other hand, with adolescence comes sexual rivalry and, with that, heightened antagonism: the driving off of rivals. If the rivals happen to be squeaks or *schwarzes*, they're driven off with extra vigour; and vice versa, no doubt.

The cozy theory that the more you see of others the more you learn to love them, or at least to tolerate them, is, alas, false. After Islington, Mr. Kawwa went on to a school in Lowestoft without a single Cypriot or coloured pupil. Asked the same questions, the Lowestoft children displayed no prejudice at all. Negroes were fine, so far as they were concerned: they didn't know any. That's the almost invariable pattern: the fewer immigrants, the greater the tolerance. What the eye doesn't see, the heart doesn't fear and resent. When they're with you in the flesh, they turn into scapegoats. If this is so, then we can expect in future more prejudice and group hostility, not less, despite all the efforts of our pastors and masters to reverse it.

3

When this Islington headmaster, himself an immigrant—his father was killed in Ireland by the British and the survivors of his family fled from Black-and-Tans—took over the school, brand-new then, three years ago, he laid down one inflexible rule: no corporal punishment. He didn't carry all his staff with him. These children are tough, unruly, and undisciplined. How can you control them without the final sanction of force?

"You go through a period of sheer chaos with each incoming batch," said the headmaster. "They don't believe there's no cane. They have to test your statement. They shout and yell and fight and make life impossible. You have to stand there and hear them call you all the four-letter words and every obscenity in the language. You've got to go on talking and whatever happens keep your temper. At first it's a nightmare for the teachers, and some of them can't take it. I don't blame them. But it's the only way. When the children grasp the fact there really *isn't* any cane, they calm down. In any case, they get tired of chaos eventually, and then you can start to talk to them like reasonable beings. It works in the end."

It certainly seemed to. The school was orderly, the children usefully employed and not carving up one another or the teachers. Yet few schools can equal this one's record for past delinquencies: 243 appearances by its pupils in the local juvenile court in three years. This was three years ago. Today the number on probation has shrunk from one hundred to nine, and discipline, based on leadership and not on fear, has been (it seems) restored.

Most Cypriot children reject the school lunch. "They'd rather go off to a café and smoke and play cards." The money? "Their parents give them plenty. One boy makes three or four pounds a week regularly on the horses. The other day I took a senior class to the Tower. I went by Underground with a packet of sandwiches, but several of the boys turned up in taxis after stopping for a slap-up luncheon on the way."

This is a school where sex instruction is given. Do the pupils need this? I wondered. "I've no doubt most of the older boys have had sex experience." Then who instructs whom? "It's a question of getting it into proportion." Only one child in ten has had church experience, however, despite a fairly high proportion of Roman Catholics, but eight out of ten (according to a questionnaire) believe in the existence of some kind of vague, mildly benevolent spiritual force like "any act of love or kindness," or "whatever you feel to be true or beautiful." There were still a few, however, who offered a suggestion that God was "a king who lives in the sky and commands an army of angels," or "an old man with a beard, a white gown, and sandals."

In contrast to the freedom they take for granted in their boys, Cypriot parents like to lock up their daughters after school. Soon this family discipline begins to chafe; daughters want to date the boys and go to coffee bars like Marilyn and Jenny. This is one reason why many Cypriot parents fear integration. They want to make their money here but not to lose their children. The children strive to integrate, the parents to prevent them from doing so.

Cypriot parents want to keep their customs, language, and identity—not to be swallowed. Can they achieve it? Older people can, certainly; with their black shawls, Orthodox services, sweet cakes, Greek tongue, they retreat into a cocoon of tight family life. (The most extreme case of the cocoon technique I heard of was a Russian woman who'd lived with her son in Leeds for thirty-five years; when the son died, the welfare people had to find a Russian interpreter because she didn't speak a word of English.)

But children can't be insulated, held back. English life sucks them away, and the parents resent it. So resistance to the host community arises, sometimes centred on the Church. In Islington the Cypriots have made an issue of the language question and the London County Council has taken on a Cypriot teacher to give instruction in Greek in one of the schools.

Almost all young children are conformers; with adolescence a contrary urge may arise. At this stage some of the adolescents join youth clubs and centres that try to keep alive a sense of national identity. Others drift away. Of the two forces, in the long run that which tends towards conformity seems almost certain to win. English life is a massive, suety, close-grained thing with great powers of absorption—like a jellyfish that enfolds in its grey, soft, caressing tentacles any rashly venturing organism and then slowly, undramatically, ingests its prey.

9. Punjab in Middlesex

In 1957 a firm of rubber manufacturers in Hayes found themselves short of labour. The atmosphere in rubber factories is hot and steamy, and now that Englishmen could pick and choose, they picked other jobs. So the firm sent to India to recruit labour, bought a few houses in the Hambrough ward of Southall to shelter them, and a problem was born.

These pioneers were Sikhs from one particular district in the Punjab. Those who followed later of their own accord came to roost with relatives, went to work in the rubber factory, scraped and saved, clubbed together and in due course bought houses, and spread out from the original focus like fungi from a spore. Now whole streets are Indian-owned, and there are probably at least 7,000 Indians and Pakistanis in Southall, owning among them about 650 houses—just over 4 percent of the total number of dwellings in the borough. Their number rises month by month, as more Asians come and as white owners sell because the district's "gone coloured." We are back again with the smell of curry, gardens used as garbage dumps or children's lavatories, dislike of outlandish foreign ways. It's said that property values in this area have dropped by 50 percent.

Now the problem has caught up with the schools. Taking the borough as a whole, it doesn't look too formidable—about 950 Asian children out of a total roll of 7,200, although that's just about 12.5 percent. (The percentage of immigrants of all kinds in the schools is 14.5.) But in certain schools the immigrants' proportion rises to about two thirds. Between them the Beaconsfield Road Infants' (nursery) and the Junior Mixed show a percentage of about 60. Six of the borough's schools carry the heaviest load.

The main difficulty has been the speed with which all this has happened. Five years ago there was scarcely an Asian child. Now each new nursery class, as it enters the stream, shows a higher immigrant proportion than the last, and the secondary schools are coming into the front line.

Not that immigrant children work their way up tidily in age groups; if they did, things would be greatly simplified. They arrive at all stages and ages. The older children must go straight into secondary schools, and none of the new arrivals knows a word of English. Special classes, special teachers, are the only answer. Such teachers have been hard to find. Starting with one experimental part-time local resident who knew some Hindi and Urdu, Southall has now gathered up twenty-one teachers, of whom four are English, two Anglo-Indian, four Pakistani, one a young Sikh from Kenya, and the rest Indians.

2

Some of their pupils are buxom damsels in pastel-shaded muslin saris or in tunics and baggy trousers, with cardigans as a concession to the English winter, who look of an age when most Indian girls would be married with a couple of babies. And, indeed, some are thought to be eighteen or even more. Their fathers have successfully pleaded with authority to let them stay on at school until they learn at least a smattering of English, when they can either get a job or cost their fathers less in marriage dowry.

Indian marriage customs, naturally, are not abandoned when a family transplants itself. A dowry has to be paid. In some distant village in the Punjab a transfer of cattle arranged in Middlesex occurs. Obviously a girl who speaks English will make a better wife in England than one who doesn't, so a bullock may be knocked off the agreed sum. I was told there was a regular schedule—a heifer off for each year's schooling, or something of that kind—but for this I can't vouch. A headmistress did, however, assure me that a school-leaver came to her radiantly one day to announce her betrothal. "Yes, a good marriage; eighteen pounds a week in Birmingham." The girl had never seen the bridegroom, and it hadn't entered her head that she should do so until after the ceremony, when he would raise her veil.

Most Sikh girls come first to school in trousers and shrink from the notion of abandoning them for physical training shorts and jerseys. But abandon them they must if they are to join with their companions in flexing knees, swinging legs, and jerking arms. No one tries to force or even to persuade them. They stand around at first looking appalled, and then wistful. Sooner or later, one by one, unobtrusively the cord is loosed, down slide the trousers, shorts replace them, and the brown-skinned little Indian joins in. So strong is the herd instinct—stronger even than parental training, if the parents are well out of sight.

"We measure the rate of integration by the trousers," a

teacher told me. "It's a great moment when they come off."
She looked around with satisfaction at the circle of her dancing, semi-integrated girls. Nut-brown legs everywhere, not a
trouser in sight. "Of course, they wouldn't do it if there were
a man in the room."

Two worlds again: beyond the asphalt, bare legs, recogni-
tion of the body, mixing of sexes, rough play, loud voices,
and pop art; in the closed circle of the Sikh family, soft
voices, respect, decorum, and modesty. The girls are docile.
"One Jamaican's more trouble in a class than ten Indians."
But the seeds of independence—or the virus of discontent,
whichever way you look at it—are being implanted. Many of
these girls will not accept, at adolescence, the suppression of
their personalities, the bridegroom they have never seen.

Last term, of the Indian girl school-leavers from a secondary modern, one went to the BBC as a translator, one to a
technical college to study science and math, one to a secretar-
ial course, one to become a machinist in a factory, and only
one to stay at home and groom herself for an arranged marriage to an unknown man.

3

In the autumn of 1963 there was trouble in Southall: indig-
nation meetings and the forming of a Residents' Association
bent on halting the flow of immigrants. The Minister of
Education went down to meet these angry citizens, and rejected their demand to segregate the children into British
and immigrant schools. His solution was to "spread the

load"—channel some of the immigrant children into schools at present almost wholly white. This affronts those parents who, while living in the "catchment area" of schools full of immigrants, have gone, and are going, to a great deal of trouble to send their offspring to white, or whiter, schools some distance away. Now it looks as if the Indians will catch up with them.

The question of tolerance, or the reverse, is closely linked to the proportion of coloured children in the schools. You could work out a graph that would hold good in most regions, districts, and boroughs: a tolerance graph, based on the proportion of immigrant children, and possibly on the speed at which the children have come in. Below a certain level—somewhere, perhaps, between 15 and 20 percent—there's no trouble; above it, restive stirrings: up in the 50 and 60 percents, unease all around. With everything there is a saturation point.

And here ideological extremes meet: those who want a form of apartheid in the schools and those prepared to die for integration. Immigrants can't integrate with natives who aren't there. They merely segregate themselves, and some of them appear to like it—at least some Indians and Pakistanis do. So integrationists and apartheid addicts unite in wishing to limit the proportion of immigrants, possibly to one third, or under, of the total roll.

The tests of integration among male Sikhs, comparable to trousers among females, are the topknot, the turban, and the beard. With their long black hair done up in a bun, their pastel-shaded, tightly folded turbans, and their soft, pretty features, to British eyes the Sikh schoolboys look just like girls. (Deceptive: Sikhs are tough, a race of fighters.) Off with turban and topknot and you've taken the first step towards relinquishing your own culture and accepting that of your hosts. Some of the Southall schoolboys have shed turbans and topknots, some have not. It's said that the Sikhs in India have sent an emissary to stiffen fathers in Britain against allowing Sikh customs to die out, and to convert the backsliders. Certainly some of the Sikh schoolboys have restored their turbans, and are re-growing their hair.

Most immigrants know that the way to keep out of trouble is to look as inconspicuous as possible, to blend into the scene. Many Sikhs in factories, therefore, have abandoned their turbans, cut their hair, and shaved their curly, well-trimmed beards. But some have stood firm. In Birmingham a sturdy character called Sang Shattar Singh enlisted as a postman and was told to shed his turban and wear a regulation cap. He refused. The dispute simmered on, the press and union took it up, and he won. Now he wears a splendid powder-blue turban and his beard is more luxuriant than ever; but he sorts letters, not delivers them, so perhaps it is a compromise. A Pakistani bus conductor has been awarded £21 1s. 10d. damages against the Bradford Corporation, which ordered him to shave his beard.

Sang Shattar Singh is justly proud of his record of nine years in the post office and never a minute late or a day lost through illness. This year he's off on holiday to Jullundur, but he's coming back. "I'm quite satisfied. The United States might have been better, but Birmingham's all right. This is my house." (It was in a slum district with poky rooms, but they were warm and dry and freshly papered; and cozily packed with people of every age from infancy to eighty; delicious smells—what's wrong with curry?—spread from the kitchen.) "My eldest son has gone to Jullundur to get a wife, then he'll return. He has a diploma in commerce from the tech. He'll start a business here."

Birmingham in 1939 had about 100 Indians, nearly all students. Today it has between 10,000 and 12,000. Seven out of ten are males. The latest arrivals are coming from East Africa, pulling out because their jobs are being Africanized. More will follow, many of them holders of British passports who bypass the controls. In any case, the controls have loopholes and byways. Ex-servicemen, for instance, get priority and jump the queue. In India and Pakistan the sale of their discharge certificates and pension books is widespread and lucrative. Employment vouchers are forged by moneylenders, who then bleed the immigrant for years. In certain British factories an immigrant can buy an offer of employment, on the firm's stationery, which enables Cousin Jamshid back in Srinagar to get his voucher under Category A (people with jobs lined up) and reach with ease this mecca of the modern economic world.

In this country there cannot now be less than 150,000 Indians and Pakistanis; there are probably more; they are coming in much faster than anyone else. Recently the Home Secretary startled everyone by announcing that well over a quarter of a million Asian vouchers had been applied for during the first year of operation of the Commonwealth Immigrants Act. Some 38,000 unskilled Asians with no jobs lined up received their vouchers; added to those in other categories, altogether some 25,700 Indians, as distinct from Pakistanis, came in. Since then their rate of arrival has been mounting. (Between July 1, 1962, and March 31, 1964, nearly 400,000 Commonwealth citizens applied for vouchers and 72,000 received them.) The population of India, let alone Pakistan, is about 450 million, and its annual increase is larger than the population of Greater London. Indians are the most fecund people on earth, and a swiftly rising Indian population will inevitably present itself in our schools.

Like West Indians, Italians, and Cypriots, most incoming Indians are peasants from villages that have scarcely changed in their essentials for centuries. Few know anything of industry, and most are illiterate. Like the Caribbeans, they settle here in family and village units which re-create the pattern that they left behind. They keep to their castes. Families of different castes will not share a house, but at work there seems to be a tacit agreement to suspend the rules: a Brahmin may work alongside say, a carpenter, or even someone lower on the scale; but Brahmins are few and far between.

Of all immigrant groups Indians and Pakistanis maintain the tightest family formations, the greatest social cohesion, the strictest moral code. Most Asian women remain encapsulated in the family circles, at once its prisoners and its queens. Asian prostitutes are rare, and you could safely offer a generous reward to any finder of a genuine female Indian teenage Beatle fan. These standards do not, however, apply to men, and the arrival of so many single males has stimulated the native easy-virtue market and in places helped to promote a recent sharp increase in venereal disease.

Indian women are tenacious of their dress. The British skirt appears to be repugnant—or perhaps indecent?—to Asian taste. An Indian teacher in a rather stuffy Midland city complained that the local education committee had passed her over for a post for which she considered herself well qualified. Racial discrimination, colour prejudice (she believed), were to blame. For her interview she had appeared before the committee in her most glamorous sari, displaying a shapely but naked midriff, eyelids kohled, hands hennaed, perfumed with Eastern essences as titivating to the senses as they were no doubt unsettling to the aldermen.

"Like you, we have our customs," hinted the local inspector of schools. "Perhaps if you'd met our committee in a plain, neat woolen suit, like one of our English applicants . . ." The Indian teacher was indignant at this slur upon her national dress; the inspector, for his part, was unable to pass on to her a remark made to him by one of her pupils, to whom he'd sat next while listening to her taking a class. Her teaching methods were fine, but the boy wasn't interested. He gave the inspector a sharp prod in the ribs with his elbow and whispered, "Eh, maister, I can see her belly, can you?"

4

Must immigrants give up their customs if they want to integrate? It appears so. This is a price not many adult Indians seem as yet prepared to pay. Their habit of living in enclosed family units enables them to live a life apart. And the indifference, and sometimes antagonism, they sense, or experience, in their hosts accentuates the tendency. Only at the workbench or in the grocers' do paths need to cross. Communication can be limited to nodding as you clock in and asking the price of tomatoes—even that isn't necessary at the supermarket, where everything is priced. Except among a small business and professional class the language barrier is deep and wide.

Women attend the clinics to have their babies weighed and

get diet sheets. This aspect of the welfare state quickly catches on. So, without exception, do family allowances: a new, almost miraculous, and wholly desirable practice in the eyes of all immigrant women. Several health authorities now print their diet sheets in Urdu, Gujarati, and Hindi. "The Indian women's eyes light up," a health visitor said, "when they see writing they can recognize"—recognize, but not usually scan; they take the sheets home for their husbands to read aloud. Mostly these are concerned to work more fat into the diet through subsidized cod-liver oil.

Their pay is the same as the natives', and they draw the family allowances. Why don't they buy their fats like everyone else? "They're saving, saving every farthing to buy a house," a health visitor said. "They come with nothing, and they're not used to our things; I've seen them living in a room so bare I've lent them a cup and a spoon to start them off, and that's literally all they've had. Eventually they'll get their house and let off beds at fifty shillings each, and then they've got an income. Meanwhile they'll buy nothing but their bare subsistence. They take the remains of last night's supper to the canteen."

Most of their own food they buy from Indian grocers, who fill a social function as well as a commercial one. Wholesalers in London import spices, pulses, rice, oils, and all the mysterious ingredients of curries, and the Indian grocer takes them round by van; he's probably a kinsman, and not only a purveyor but a courier, newspaper, antenna, employment agent, and adviser as well. He's part of the closed circuit of Indian life, pausing for a chat and a sweet drink or cup of tea in each of his customers' and kinsmen's reception rooms. Despite the high value of each cubic foot of space every Indian house, unlike those of Pakistanis, must have its reception room, where guests can be greeted—like everything else, shared.

Shared with one another—with the kinship group, mainly; beyond that, with the community. With the British, no. Host and immigrant pursue their separate ways. Socially and culturally there's so little to share. Not language. Not religion. Sikh temples spring up everywhere—one in Birmingham, one in Smethwick, one in Leeds, one in Southall, others elsewhere. Not values, food, or dress. Indian films are shown on Sundays, Indian houses packed with Indians, Indian youth clubs formed, Indian workers' associations started. Neither side really wants to mingle. We don't want to gulp them, they don't want to be swallowed.

To tolerate each other, politely if possible, seems to be the aim. We need Indian labour, they need British cash: a strictly business arrangement. It's when the two communities become, willy-nilly, socially entangled, as in the schools, that the buds of discord unfold.

10. Uprooted Men

It looks in winter like a bit of landscape on the moon, or what I've always imagined the moon to be like: bleak, cold, grey, and desolate, with a nasty biting wind and no sunshine, dead flat. It's the craters, I suppose, you see on lunar photographs; there are craters here, too. They're called knotholes, and from them clay has been scooped and loaded into tublike steel wagons to proceed in slow, funereal processions to the kilns whose tall and tapering chimneys sprout like clusters of enormous candles from the Bedfordshire plain.

For centuries bricks have been made here—not even straw, apparently, has to be added, it's such a simple process; but a process demanding (despite mechanization) heavy, cold, wet work out of doors and heavy, hot work firing kilns inside; and mainly piecework, so you have to keep hard at it, no playing crown-and-anchor behind crates. If you *do* work hard, you can make up to twenty pounds a week, but in the motor-works at Luton the pay is higher, the hours are shorter, and conditions more congenial. So the natives are unwilling, and early in the fifties several brick companies recruited labour in Italy, which started Bedford's Italian colony.

For some years the largest brickworks, which turns out ten million bricks a week, employed well over 1,000 Italians at any given time, not to mention Irish, Yugoslavs, Poles, and men of other nations. Aliens are bound to their type of employment for four years; after that they're free to get any job they please. The Italians, as their four years expire, are leaving almost to a man and getting easier, better jobs or setting up in business on their own. Most of them have bought houses, prospered, and are "upwardly mobile" in a big way.

As they go, in come Pakistanis. At the moment, the company employs about equal numbers of each, but this year Pakistanis are coming into the lead. The next-largest group, a long way behind, are Yugoslavs, then Irish, then Indians, West Indians, and Poles. In all, twenty-four nationalities are on the labour roll, and on the production side only one in three is home-born. There are even two Arabs.

This is almost a textbook example of what is happening all over the country if for Italians you read Caribbeans. Two years ago it was the Caribbean influx that was in the news; more than 62,000 came in during 1961, and 43,000 Asians, almost equally divided between Pakistan and India. In the latest period nearly three times as many came from the Indian subcontinent as from the Caribbean. Nothing like as many Asians came as wanted to, but the numbers who actually got their vouchers (38,000) exceeded those who even applied from the rest of the Commonwealth put together.

Compared with the Caribbean immigrants who once so colourfully erupted in our London termini with banjos, straw hats, bright silk shirts, and bundles of yams, the Pakistanis are a more prosaic, earnest lot. They bring no musical instruments and don't sing, carouse, dance, wear hats at jaunty angles, or frequent dubious clubs. They are, of course,

Muslims, who shouldn't take a drink—if they do it's with a sense of sin, not relaxation—or mix with women socially, and the only clubs they join are likely to be burial societies, to make sure they will lie with heads towards Mecca, should the Reaper strike them down in a foreign land.

Except for a few ship-jumpers, most come by air in rather sad, depressed, bewildered huddles of males, understanding not a word of the language, totally ignorant of what this sunless, noisy, crowded world will offer them, heavily in debt for their passages and passports, which are sometimes forged and nearly always bribed for, and terribly homesick for the families they've left behind.

A roof, a job. The first is not too difficult because plenty of Pakistanis are here already—the High Commissioner's estimate is one *lakh,* or 100,000. Newcomers go straight to a kinsman or a fellow villager. Generally they carry an address on a slip of paper, and it's not unusual for a pedestrian in a Midland city to find a thin brown hand clutching a crumpled missive thrust under his eyes with a mute appeal for help. Immigrants from East Pakistan, who speak Bengali, will lodge with other easterners; not merely that, but perhaps with fellow villagers from (say) Habiganj, not rubbing shoulders or sharing curries with unreliable characters from Maulvi Bazar. Those from West Pakistan, Urdu-speakers, will gravitate to households originating in the same district of the Punjab.

2

Most of these new arrivals will find themselves in one of those bachelor establishments the Pakistanis have made peculiarly their own. Here a single man will pay from twenty to fifty shillings a week[1] for a dormitory bed to be shared, most likely with a night-shift worker if he himself works by day. Twenty or thirty men may be crammed into one house: as a rule, a rather slummy house in Stepney or Bradford, Smethwick or Balsall Heath. The lodgers cook their own communal curry when they get home from work. The ratio of Pakistani women to men in Britain is estimated at one in ten—in Stepney, one in twenty. Men with wives are *ipso facto* well-to-do, mostly either professionals like doctors and lawyers, in business on their own—there are at least five hundred Pakistani restaurants in Britain—or in middle-class types of employment.

No unskilled Pakistani worker—and nine out of ten are said to be unskilled—can bring his wife. For one thing, he can't possibly afford it: he's sold and pledged and mortgaged everything he's got to come himself; the whole object of the exercise is to make enough to pay back expenses, send money to his family, and buy a plot of land at home and build a house. Since Muslim customs rigidly preclude his wife's going out to work, she's bound to be an economic liability, not an asset as Jamaican wives are. Added to that, any Pakistani who

1 $2.80 to $7.00 at current rate of exchange.

does import his family must provide a much higher standard of accommodation than a West Indian needs to. He must have a separate kitchen and lavatory and at least two bedrooms, one for the couple, one for the children, and a third when the sexes separate, at six or so. So wives and families are strictly for the rich—a status symbol. A few make do with English wives, not nearly so expensive, as they are prepared to work and, not being Muslims, permitted to do so; but, while often personally respected, as a class they are looked upon by the community, according to the sociologist Mr. Hamza Alavi, as "a betrayal of the family in Pakistan."

Nor are temporary liaisons favoured because of the expense; generally it costs more to keep a mistress, who needs to be pleased and seldom goes out to work, than a wife. So most Pakistanis must choose between celibacy and resort to prostitutes; this is looked upon as venial, and no doubt accounts for the community's high incidence of venereal disease. In Bradford, for example, a Pakistani stronghold, it is one hundred times higher among coloured immigrants than among the natives.

3

In most of these dormitory houses a figure exists whose status and authority seem, to those English who penetrate into off-duty Pakistani lives, somewhat mysterious and shadowy. Often a "boss man" or "big uncle" collects everyone's rent, conducts any dealings that may be needed with authority, and exercises a rather nebulous control over his fellow lodg-

ers. He may be the senior elder of a family, or a man of some
position in a distant village. As he is often elderly and non-
English-speaking, from an English point of view he is seldom
the best intermediary, but that can't be helped.

How to fill their leisure time is the lodgers' major problem. There's nowhere to go and nothing to do. On weekends
those who are literate write long letters home for their illiterate fellows as well as for themselves. They play cards. Now
and again there's an Indian or Pakistani film. A few of the
younger men play football, and that's about all. They don't
dance. The pub is out—not only for religious reasons, but
because the driving force behind these uprooted men is all to
save, save, save. A few fall from grace; there's even a Pakistani
in Leeds who keeps a pub, but most of these are men who
came before the rush, as seamen, and settled here. That's why
so many of the newcomers have come to Stepney; a small
community of seafarers already established there acted as a
nucleus. The majority of Stepney Pakistanis, numbering perhaps 10,000, come from a district called Sylhet, where the
prewar seafarers originated.

The incentive to put in as much overtime as possible is
strong. This naturally endears the Pakistanis to their employers, who also give them high marks for timekeeping,
willingness, and docility. Perhaps their main drawback as employees is their all but total ignorance of English, and sometimes poor physique. Tuberculosis among Pakistanis in
Bradford, for example, is forty times more common than in
the British population as a whole. About half of those subsequently found to be infected arrive with the disease already
diagnosable. These could be weeded out by X-ray before they
come, and save themselves and everyone else a lot of misery
and trouble.

A Pakistani doctor I talked to couldn't understand why this wasn't done. "I nearly went to Canada," he said, "and applied for a passport, and I had to have a chest X-ray first. I had no objection; why should I? It seemed extremely sensible. The British should insist on it too." It's quite untrue, he added, that Pakistanis come here to take advantage of the health and other welfare services. "They come to make money, and they can't do that if they're on national assistance. The trouble is the other way round. They're so desperately anxious to keep up their remittance payments, they'll conceal their symptoms and go to almost any length to avoid being sent to hospital."

4

Pakistanis seem to believe that the way to keep out of trouble is to avoid as far as possible all contact with the natives, except at work. The absence of women makes such contacts much harder to establish. Enormous differences in custom, outlook, and intention divide the two communities. Perhaps the deepest is religion. Attendance at the mosques—in London, one each in Stepney, Regents' Park, and Putney—is poor, but that is because on Fridays everyone's at work.

Couldn't services be switched to Sundays? There was an emphatic shaking of heads. "Quite impossible." On the other hand, eight Pakistanis out of ten are said to observe the one-month daytime fast of Ramadan; in the absence of the traditional gunfire to mark start and finish, notices appear in the Pakistani papers published in London: *Desher Daak,* a fortnightly in Bengali, and *Inquilab* and *Mashriq,* both in Urdu. Few of the faithful will eat in factory canteens for fear of encountering sausages, bacon, or pork.

Internally the Pakistani community is deeply riven, both geographically, between East and West, and socially, between a thin top crust of highly educated and the peasant mass. No one could be more sophisticated, intelligent, articulate, and civilized than the educated Pakistani diplomats and doctors, professors and barristers—a small world but a choice one, adorned by graceful, charming wives. I spent a riveting afternoon with a flashing-eyed Pakistani who had been a major at twenty-one. Napoleon had been his hero, to become a military conqueror his aim. Ruler of a province holding 300,000 people at twenty-five, he'd married a girl of surpassing loveliness (they talked in Persian) and loaded her with splendid jewels, lived in a princely state of exaltation until he'd tasted bitter fruit, relinquished everything, given away his possessions, abandoned his faith, and wandered as a beggar; he probed the religions of the world to solve the insoluble, returned to Islam, and dedicated the rest of his life—he is still under forty—to the welfare of his people. Now he serves them in a useful but unspectacular capacity in an industrial city, dealing with mundane problems of accommodation, permits, and threatened strikes. It was like listening to a chapter read from *The Arabian Nights.*

Other educated Pakistanis, less glamorous if just as dedicated, meet in a poky, low-ceilinged room in a back street in Stepney, shabbier, dirtier, and more sordid than anything in Dickens' London. Though it has been condemned for demolition, no one is even trying to stop the place from sinking into a slough of decay. Filthy bits of paper driven by an icy wind flap about in muddy gutters, feeble street lights half illuminate piles of garbage, every window is encrusted with grime. If it weren't for the Pakistanis, crowding into these human warrens because they can buy them for next to nothing, the hovels would be gone by now.

Here the committee of the Pakistani Welfare Association, all unpaid, organize a panel of doctors working in London hospitals who come down to Stepney once a week, in their spare time, to examine anyone who asks for help and write down his symptoms in English for his National Health Service doctor to read. There's also a panel of barristers who advise about such matters as leases and come to the aid of anyone they hear of who's in trouble with the law.

5

Pakistanis are believed to save about one third of their earnings; on a modest estimation that works out at almost twenty million pounds a year. In London alone they are said to have bought at least 1,000 houses. Most of their savings have to be converted into rupees and sent home. What with the naïveté in matters of banking of most of the savers and the astuteness of the Indian moneylending class, quite a lot of this cash disappears on the way. So a group of Pakistani businessmen have started an enterprise called Anglopak to remit the money to the men's families at the best rates of exchange and use the sterling balances to buy things Pakistan needs, thus helping both the toiling immigrants and their nation's trade balance, chronically in need of repair. They also hope, if all goes well, to advance money to Pakistani immigrants for buying houses.

But not to settle in forever; most Pakistanis want to go home. At present few intend to send for their wives; they pull around their ears their religion, customs, and village associations, sharing news and hopes and even, as we've seen, rooms and beds, and huddle in this warm enclosure; their contacts with their hosts are minimal.

And yet a great many undoubtedly will stay, including some of the most successful. I met one such in Bradford, a grocer who owns a small chain of even smaller grocery stores, but evidently profitable ones; he'd just taken his wife and son on holiday to Pakistan in two cars, shipped by sea, driving 6,000 miles and then returning; he said the trip cost him £3,000. He has settled permanently in England, but then he has an English wife and so is not typical.

Most Pakistanis save, go home, return to Britain for a second penance, and hope by then to have put by enough to bid farewell forever to our frigid welcome, chilly climate, and alien ways. It remains to be seen whether that hope will be realized. At present so few bother to attend weekend classes, available in various Pakistani strongholds, to teach colloquial English that most of these classes have had to close down. For the time being, anyway, the only thing most Pakistanis want from us is the money they earn.

11. Clocking In

"EVERY immigrant who's in employment has work-mates who've helped him and taught him his job." This was from an Englishman employed in Birmingham to smooth out points of friction between immigrants and hosts. "There's a colossal amount of goodwill among our people to set against the kicks now and then."

A Pakistani in east London said, "I've got a steady job, a skilled glass blower, good pay. When I came, I knew nothing. In the trade there's a five-year apprenticeship, you're not allowed to join the union till you've completed it. I learned the job in six months. The others helped me." "And the union—didn't they mind?" "It was the other way. After three years they considered my application and let me join; they waived the rules. Everyone helped me." He added, "But I'm the only skilled Pakistani working for the firm."

One tends, as always, to hear only about trouble: when strikes occur either by British workers protesting against immigrants or by immigrants in arms against some slight, real or fanciful. Since the war about 1.2 million people have immigrated here from other lands. They haven't all stayed, but most have. The number of Commonwealth immigrants, almost wholly coloured, registered for work has more than doubled since 1959, and is still rising. It's reckoned that by 1963 Britain had not far short of three quarters of a million postwar Commonwealth immigrants. Nearly all the workers among these were employed. Roughly speaking, eight out of every thousand of our labour force are immigrants, not counting the Irish.

This hardly bears out the theory that we've become so dependent on immigrants that we couldn't carry on without them. But of course they aren't evenly distributed. They plug holes. The most obvious one—we can all see it—is in public transport. "They run the buses." It's quite true that most public transport authorities would be up a tree without them, and a lot of buses would come off the road. In Bradford about one third, in Birmingham one fifth, of the bus drivers and conductors are coloured immigrants.

London Transport is one of the country's largest employers of immigrant, and especially of Caribbean, labour, but it doesn't keep any figures to distinguish between immigrant and native staff. It started the ball rolling in 1956 with a mission to Barbados to explain its needs and set up machinery, in collaboration with the Barbados Government, for supplying them. The island's government advanced passage money to successful applicants, and the Transport Board helped to find accommodations in London, trained them, and guaranteed jobs. Recruits had to measure up to the same standards as native Englishmen who turned up at the recruiting centre in the Marylebone Road: that is to say, they had to be literate, healthy, and equal to a simple aptitude test.

This scheme has been successful; failures have been few, and most Barbadians have stuck to their jobs. Altogether about 3,000 have been absorbed, apart from those recruited in London in the ordinary way. British Railways, several regional hospital boards, and the British Hotels and Restaurants Association have also brought in Barbadians under this official scheme. (Barbados is the most densely populated of all the British Caribbean islands.) London Transport's operational staff on Underground and buses stands at around 47,000 men and women. No one knows the proportion of immigrants, but if it is the same as Birmingham's—that is, one fifth—this means employment for over 9,000 immigrants. The work may not bring in a fortune—though nowadays the wages aren't too poor—but it's steady, carries sick pay, pensions, canteen facilities and other extras, and you get about and see the streets of London. The immigrants like it, on the whole.

2

West Indian women are coming over in increasing numbers, and most look out for jobs, part-time if they have small children. They'll take on almost anything except domestic work in private households. Employers welcome them, but say that they are slow to learn, alert for slights, and sometimes aggressive towards their British co-workers. The co-workers are inclined at first to lodge complaints about outlandish foreign ways, like taking queer foods in thermos flasks to the washroom instead of using the canteen, or eating Kit-e-Kat sandwiches. (This story crops up again and again, like keeping chickens in the bath.)

"It's not a colour bar, it's just that it takes our people time to get used to anything different, and the Jamaicans don't always understand our ways," said a welfare officer in Birmingham whose firm has employed West Indian women—about one in ten of the female labour force—for six or seven years. "We've had no serious trouble, and on the whole, they mix in well. They all like pop music. But they're awful babies. The least injury, and you'd think the world was coming to an end. They don't like change, anything new; if one of them is moved to another machine, quite often she'll develop a pain in the foot or an ache in the arm. And they pounce like cats on the least chance of compensation."

Some indulge in "blemishing," a well-known practice among West Indians in the Midlands. Either you play up to the limit, and beyond, for a slight injury or, like an old soldier, you create one: scratch a hand, slash a finger, stub a toe. Then you hope for compensation. The West Indians' hopes are seldom satisfied, but they go on trying and bear no grudge when they fail.

Many employers, though few will admit this, keep to a rough quota for coloured workers, generally about 10 percent. They say they do this to avoid trouble with their English workers. Some firms risk a much larger number. The overall percentage of Indians and Pakistanis employed in Bradford's textile mills is 20, and some individual firms employ four Asians out of five operators. The damp heat of the woolen mills, it's said, suits the Asians, and they're to be found also, in considerable numbers, in the foundries. Here the work is much heavier, and only the fittest stand the pace.

If some of our factories would close down without immigrants, so would some hospitals, or at any rate, wards. In a Midland city the staff of a geriatric hospital with over 1,000 beds is 60 percent coloured. The mental and geriatric hospitals and wards are much more dependent on immigrants than are the general hospitals. "We get pushed into the jobs the whites don't want," is a comment often heard.

It's true that these are the least sought-after branches of nursing. Since we haven't enough nurses to go round, someone has to go short, and generally it's the mentally sick and bedridden old. As relatively few immigrants have the educational background to qualify for the State Register, relatively more find their way into hospitals and wards with a high ratio of nursing aides and orderlies to full-blown staff nurses and sisters. More still find work on the domestic side as ward-maids, kitchen staff, and the like.

But more and more girls from Commonwealth countries are coming here as student nurses: at present over 12,000 are in training in our hospitals, out of a total of 54,000—more than one student in five. Many of these will go back to their countries of origin, especially the West Africans; but nearly six out of every ten coloured student nurses are West Indians, and (let's hope) many of these will stay. They'd better, or the plight of our hospitals will grow even more desperate than it is now. No one knows what proportion of the 322,425 nurses at present on the State Register are immigrants, but roughly one in eight of the 15,000 admitted (on average) annually were trained abroad, not necessarily in the Commonwealth. This is in addition to overseas students who are trained here.

Just under 18,000 whole-time, fully qualified doctors and dentists are employed in our hospitals, of whom about 3,000 (an estimate) were born overseas. Not, of course, all coloured; there are many Australians, some Canadians and New Zealanders, and a number of Hitler refugees.

It's a different story when it comes to the younger doctors of the grade of registrar and under, the coming men and women. No less than 42 percent of these, working in our hospitals, were born overseas, and more than half—52 percent—of those in nonteaching hospitals outside London. It wouldn't be correct to call them all immigrants, because many are postgraduate students. However, it's certainly true to say that we couldn't treat our sick today in our hospitals without the services of doctors born overseas.

3

If the shortage grows worse, we might even have to try to recruit overseas nurses and doctors, like the Caribbean bus conductors, Italian brickworkers, or Italian coal miners who arrived in 1952. Although the National Union of Mineworkers lacked enthusiasm for this project, the shortage of coal miners was then so pressing that their permission was won, and 2,400 young Italians were brought over, placed in hostels, and briefly trained.

The British miners didn't like it. Despite the labour shortage a quarter of the Italians never even got down a mine; some were repatriated, some went off to dig Belgian coal, and less than half stayed on for any length of time. Five years later the number had dwindled to under 700, and no more were brought in.

Then there was the Hungarian fiasco. The aftermath of the abortive Budapest rising in October 1956 expelled over the Austrian border more than 100,000 refugees—homeless, hungry, destitute. After some shilly-shallying our own government lowered the immigration barriers, and in a little over three weeks about 11,500 refugees swept in. A camp near Rugeley accommodated several thousand, other centres were hastily improvised, houses commandeered. Voluntary services swung into action with the enthusiasm such crises always evoke. This left us all a little breathless; barriers went up again, and the flow was halted to a trickle. By the end of 1957 it had virtually ceased. By then over 21,000 Hungarians had come in.

After getting them all into camps and hostels, the next step was to get them out again. No one wanted to freeze them in a "hostel mentality." For their part, they nearly all wanted to go to North America. Some 5,500 were quickly handed on to Canada, but the Canadians had other sources of supply and the rest of the Hungarians had to settle for a land at once closer to the Russians and less well endowed with opportunity. Most of the refugees were young, fit men whom industry was glad to welcome, despite their lack of English. Some left the country, but in all about 14,500 remained. By the end of 1957 nearly all had moved out of hostels, into the mainstream of British life.

Nearly all, that is, except for 3,561 brought from Austria by the National Coal Board, plus another 630 recruited in Britain from hostels and camps. Still, perhaps, shaken by the Italians, the National Union of Mineworkers agreed to this humane gesture—and not only humane, for we had remained short of coal miners—with the proviso that the permission of each local branch must be given before a single Hungarian was lowered down a pit.

The Coal Board put the Hungarians into hostels and holiday camps, paid them, and gave them a twelve-week course in English and a little elementary training. (Only about one third had previously been miners.) Then came the moment for them to start work. At almost every colliery the union's local branches—the sturdy British withers of their members unwrung by the refugees' plight—refused their permission. The Coal Board's representatives pleaded in vain. Out of 4,200 Hungarian would-be miners only 821 ever got down a pit. Industrial jobs were found for the remainder. So the coal mines never got their infusion of new blood, and the mineworkers' union added no lustre to its name.

Time, perhaps, mellowed its attitude, or perhaps dark-complexioned Commonwealth citizens are thought to be more deserving than anti-Communist refugees; no objections have been voiced, at least openly, to the employment at the Gedling Colliery in Nottingham of some 150 West Indians in a labour force some 2,250 strong.

4

Hot on Hungarian heels came the Anglo-Egyptians, a pathetic assortment of victims, all British subjects, of the Suez debacle of November 1956. Summarily expelled by President Nasser, they arrived from Egypt in bedraggled family groups with nothing but the clothes they stood up in, leaving behind them sequestered property to the value of between thirty-five and forty million pounds and everything they couldn't carry away at less than twenty-four hours' notice—cars in the garage, silver on the tables, dresses in the wardrobe, money in the bank. Most had been well-to-do, some rich, nearly all middle class in habit, used to Cairo's easy living in comfortable flats, its office jobs, luxuries, and servants. Many were elderly, some old, unfit, and ill suited to the hostels into which they had to be thrust in the middle of an English winter.

About 8,000 of them came. As objects of British sympathy the Hungarians who had challenged Russian tanks in Budapest quite overshadowed these disheartened, unheroic Levantines, undone by the ignominious failure of a British enterprise of which, in any case, many Britons were ashamed. Few spoke English or knew anything of English ways. Most of them were, in origin, Maltese, and spoke a bastard Italian. The government gave £100,000 to the Anglo-Egyptian Aid Society, a small voluntary body which coped in an atmosphere of crisis and frustration until an official body, the Anglo-Egyptian Resettlement Board, took over early in 1957.

By then some of the refugees were in hostels and the rest were keeping body and soul together with allowances from the National Assistance Board. Those prepared to face another plunge into the unknown, and young and fit enough to do so, went to Australia—1,200 of them by the end of 1957. A further 1,000 or so found jobs in Britain. The rest remained disconsolately in hostels, lodgings, and cheap hotels, their roots torn up and all their savings, possessions, and security gone.

Compensation was the big issue. The British Government excelled itself in stalling, arguing, and cheeseparing. Eventually it settled, including loans to be repaid, for somewhere in the region of ten million pounds. After prolonged wrangling the Egyptian Government set aside 27.5 million pounds to be paid over to the unfortunate people, surely innocent of any crime, it had so summarily expelled.

They were not easy to place in employment. An accordion player from an Alexandria nightclub proved especially hard to integrate. Today, more than seven years after Suez, two hostels accommodate a residue of old and unemployable at Leamington and Harrow. At Stonehouse, in Gloucestershire, a rather sad little colony arose because the local council had some unused houses into which they could be moved. There they remain, far from any centre of employment which could use such skills as they possess or train them in new ones. The remainder have vanished into English life. Their children are growing up, or have grown up, as English children—integrated.

12. A Toe on the Ladder

IT'S COMMONLY said that the rate of unemployment among immigrants is higher than among their British comrades. To judge by sample surveys, this appears to be true.

A survey carried out in Leeds showed three times as many immigrants as natives out of work. Nottingham has an exceptionally low unemployment rate: in October 1963, a fraction over 1.8 percent. (Almost wholly male: virtually all employable women were working.) Among coloured immigrants the rate was 9 percent.

Discrimination? By and large, probably not. Almost all the immigrants arrive unskilled; there's always a batch who've just come and await openings; nowadays most new arrivals understand no English, and so their choice of jobs is very limited. Some unemployables arrive who should never have come. I heard of one old Pakistani of nearly seventy with double cataract, another with a crippled leg, both on national assistance, presumably for life. Some have been on the rolls for several years.

Even these unemployables came here, I was assured, for the old, old reason—streets lined with gold. Generally there's a son or married daughter who will take them in. Agents who advance passage money, the sharks and predators, spread these rumours, embellish these dreams. The suckers are bitterly disillusioned. No one will advance them passage money to get them home, and there's no hope of saving it. They're trapped, and we pay.

"Employers," said the manager of a labour exchange, "look to the man and not the colour; what they want is good labour; where it comes from doesn't interest them." A sociologist qualified this. "If two men are equally suitable, the one who's white will get the job." Both agreed that employers had stuck faithfully to the union rule about seniority: last come, first out, regardless of race or hue.

Prejudice can't be discounted, but it seems more often to be fear of prejudice among the public that actuates the employer than his indulgence in it. (Of course, this could be an excuse.) Rightly or wrongly, some caterers and managers of stores believe the public dislikes to see coloured people handling food. Why should housewives object (if they do) to receiving a packet of cornflakes from a pair of dusky hands, but not to another pair performing far more intimate services for them in the hospital? Put their lives in the hands of a coloured doctor or bus driver, accept a postman or ticket collector, but not, it seems, or with reluctance, a meter reader, teacher, or policeman? Is it because there lingers deep in many minds the old colonial conviction, going back to the days of slavery, that the right and fitting tasks for darker brethren are those of the servant, not of the master? This path beckons into forests of psychology and behaviour where we cannot now follow; the gnarled roots of colour prejudice go very deep, thrusting down below the sunny courts of reason.

2

West Indians, especially, have complained that they can get a job all right but when it comes to promotion they are passed over. "The British, they'll accept you as a mate but not a boss." Is this true?

There are charge hands in factories, R.A.F. sergeants, foremen of building gangs—immigrants with a toe on the lowest rung of the ladder. So far as I could learn, no inspectors on buses, guards on passenger trains, prison officers, building site foremen, bank cashiers, factory or chain store managers—the list is long. Definitely no regular policemen.

Employers and others who do the promoting point out that few immigrants have been long enough in jobs in Britain to qualify for advancement. The great majority have come only within the last five years or so, and may have moved around a bit before they settled down. Quite soon an appreciable number will have had sufficient length of service to justify a rise in status. Will they get it? That will be the crucial test. Wait and see.

Employers also say it's no use pushing on too far ahead of public opinion; and public opinion, while not, as a rule, actively unfriendly to the immigrants, isn't ready to accept them in positions of authority. Or even if most public opinion *is* ready—a moot point—there's enough opinion that isn't to stir up trouble, a thing no one wants. The racial issue may seem calm enough on the surface, but it's a very hot potato, and people are handling it with asbestos gloves.

This issue of promotion most affects the Caribbeans because nearly all are wage earners, with little ambition to set up on their own. Pakistanis are perhaps the least concerned because so many mean to go home. Many Indians, like the Italians, Cypriots, and Poles, intend to pull out of the whole wage-earning system by starting up in business on their own. Catering, moneylending, and door-to-door sales are popular lines. Indian building contractors have been sighted in the Hebrides.

A welfare worker in the Midlands who sorts out immigrants' problems, from buying Muslim burial grounds to getting diet sheets for diabetics translated into Urdu, said, "Coloured immigrants with skills, white-collar ones expecially, *do* come up against race prejudice. An experienced accountant showed me a pile of rejections he'd received to applications for a job. An Indian with a B.S. in chemistry was turned down by a firm that was advertising for men with his qualifications; they told him it wasn't their policy to employ immigrants who might have to be sent overseas."

What is the trade union attitude toward all this? "Ambivalent to the point of schizophrenia," remarks sociologist Sheila Patterson in *Dark Strangers,* her study of West Indians in Brixton. And long ago summed up by Ben Tillett in his observation to the Jews, "You are our brothers and we'll do our duty by you, but we wish you hadn't come."

At the top it's crystal-clear: at any price, no colour bar. Trade union leaders have stuck to this gun from the start and not wavered. But what's propounded at Transport House or passed with acclamation in Scarborough and what goes on at floor level in the factories are different things. "They take our jobs." The hind legs and the front legs of the donkey proceed in opposite directions, and the skin barely holds. What strains it (apart from seniority) is, in the opinion of many, simply numbers—too many coloured immigrants in one place at one time. As in the schools, there's a plimsoll line of safety.

In Nottingham, a few years back, the president of the local branch of the woodworkers' union was a Caribbean. One of two Indian candidates have stood, so far without success, in local government elections. A couple of years ago the first coloured magistrate was appointed to an English bench: Mr. Eric Irons of Nottingham, one of the pioneer West Indians who came first to Britain in the R.A.F., returned after the war, married, and settled down; now he works in the city's department of education and takes a full part in local life. So not all doors are closed. Nor is it all a British fault that more haven't been pushed open. As we've seen, many Asian immigrants hold themselves aloof. Even Caribbeans are not good mixers at the institutional level. On a personal basis, yes. But unions, meetings, politics, societies, evening classes—most of them pass these up. Partly this may be just indifference and idleness, partly an instinct to keep out of trouble by staying in the undergrowth: not hiding, but not strutting, either. No point in thrusting yourself forward, sticking out your neck. English politics, English unions, are for English people, not for immigrants. But if they got a warmer welcome, perhaps they'd join in more.

3

Ten years ago a few dozen Chinese restaurants thrived in London and the major cities. Then, unobtrusively, they started to crop up in all sorts of unlikely places, and now a thick rash of them covers the land.

You expect them in London and find plenty—walk down the King's Road and you can see them winking at you seductively on every side, as thick as fairy lanterns at a fete. What is more unexpected is to find them in places like Bradford, Swindon, Abergavenny, and Scunthorpe. It's strange to see a solid Yorkshire joint-and-two-veg businessman going off to the Pearl of the Orient or the Queen of Canton to his chop suey or pork and ginger with fried rice. However, his eyes are apt to stray to a corner of that very long menu (and when they come, all the dishes look the same) headed English Food, where he can settle for a pork chop and chips or sausages and mash.

He gets quick service, reasonable prices, and "atmosphere" provided by a paper lantern dangling from the ceiling, a scrawl of Chinese characters, and cheap prints on the walls. And, of course, by the inscrutable Oriental waiters, who appear to speak no English and yet understand what you say.

They really *are* inscrutable; no one seems to know anything about them, and they won't say. There's a pleasing theory that they are spies planted here after the Chinese break with Russia disorganized Red China's intelligence services. This could be a rumour started to thicken the atmosphere of Oriental mystery, in case the paper lanterns aren't enough.

Most of the proprietors and waiters come from Hong Kong, a few from Malaysia. No figures seem to be kept about the numbers who arrive or where they go. In Leeds, for a while, they headed the list of new arrivals in terms of numbers. (Twenty a month.) There's an Association of Chinese Restaurateurs in London, but its membership fluctuates from month to month because new restaurants keep opening up and old ones closing down. A guess is between 1,500 and

2,000. If each one employs five men, that accounts for nearly 10,000 Chinese.

In Lancaster Gate there's a Hong Kong office where Mr. Woo—formerly an inspector of schools in Hong Kong and now a liaison officer with Hong Kong Chinese in Britain—told me that there are thought to be 45,000 Chinese in Britain, of whom about 30,000 come from Hong Kong. In addition there are about 1,600 Hong Kong university students here, including some 400 student nurses.

"These restaurants," he said thoughtfully, "most of their owners, you know, are not restaurateurs at all. They are peasants, very poor. Hong Kong is dreadfully overcrowded—over three million people in a little cluster of islands not much bigger than your Isle of Ely. I met a friend of mine the other day from Hong Kong. He was a police inspector there; now he has a restaurant. He doesn't know anything about restaurants, but he's a clever man. Once a Chinese gets his restaurant started, he sends for his relations to be waiters. They live in dormitories and save money until they can send for their wives. Then those who can find an opening start up on their own.

"Saturation point must soon be reached," Mr. Woo added. "There's so much competition. On the Continent they have stopped the Chinese—some waiters who went from London for a holiday in Holland were turned back. They don't want any more Chinese."

What about other occupations? Mr. Woo shook his head. "No openings." Years ago there were Chinese laundries everywhere. What's become of them? Mr. Woo shook his head again. "Who knows?"

We talked about rice. A look of pain passed over Mr. Woo's open countenance when we touched on English methods. "We cook it differently," he said with restraint. "We never pour away *any* water. To us, that seems. . ." Words failed.

London is full of little shops which purvey Chinese food. As you enter, you are engulfed in a consortium of odours in which dried and pickled fish predominate. Open barrels full of a black, glutinous substance—soybean, I think, boiled and pounded—stand by the door. What about shark's fins? The owner, or assistant, a short, broad, ebullient young man from Hong Kong, roared with laughter. "Too expensive! Four shillings an ounce!"

I asked him if he liked London. He roared with laughter. "Lonely," he said. "My friends work in restaurants at night. No one talk!" Two sloe-eyed girls arranging tins in the back of the shop exploded with merriment. "This man never lonely," one of them volunteered. Had he his family with him? "I not married! I never marry, not me. . ."

This brought the house down. One of the girls rushed up to him and flung her arms round his neck. "Having many, many girl friends," she cried between bouts of laughter. "In London, in Paris, Germany, America, all over." They were convulsed. This was the merriest group of immigrants I came across. I bought a bottle of soy sauce and left them rocking with hilarity among the salted fish, bamboo shoots, and sacks of rice.

13. Through Dark Glasses

IN Paddington there's a Barbadian who thought, when she arrived two years ago, that everyone in London went to church every Sunday in St. Paul's. Disillusionment was bitter—not merely the fact that you can't pack them all into St. Paul's, but that very few Londoners, though well supplied with edifices, ever enter a church at all.

"I can't enjoy my church here, the church so cold and empty and nobody sing." Churches in the West Indies are places where you convivially foregather and make friends and sing. West Indians expect the same of ours—the mother church to them. (The majority are Protestants, many of the Methodist persuasion.) Here, they believe, if nowhere else, they'll feel themselves enfolded, needed, desired.

"The West Indian wants to feel wanted," remarks the Reverend Clifford Hill in his gloomy survey, *West Indian Migrants and the London Churches*. Alas, they have been nurtured in a creed outworn: that of the mother country who loves and cherishes her colonial young and sets them an impeccable example in Christian living. Some Jamaicans who have travelled, or at least seen motion pictures and observed how tourists behave, are less naïve; but folk from smaller islands still arrive expecting to find everything spick-and-span, clean and tidy, gay and bright and full of respectable Christians; they'll see the Queen riding by in a golden coach with prancing horses, young men playing cricket watched by elders in top hats and wedding coats, and ladies in silk dresses and white gloves pouring tea.

And then—a back street off the Harrow Road, Paddington. Grey skies, an east wind, newspaper headlines about a sex murder, hordes and hordes of unsmiling people with pale grey faces and dark grey clothes scurrying as if accursed, each one folded back on himself. Cold empty churches, cold empty hearts. "I never think London she look so old and dirty and so poor and different from the way I picture." New West Indian arrivals, as a Barbadian, Mr. F. Jeremiah, has said, "often suffer a great shock when they discover that there are English people who couldn't care less about the royal family and are not concerned about the Commonwealth."

Some are stupefied. A nursing tutor told me of a group of Bechuana girls pitchforked by air from the Kalahari's fringes into a big London hospital, who were reduced to senseless giggles and unable, for about a week, to take anything in. She thought they should go first to some cottage hospital to get acclimatized, instead of spanning in twenty-four hours not merely several thousand miles but several centuries.

2

In the British Caribbean islands, according to the Reverend Clifford Hill, seventy men and women out of every hundred go regularly to church. But to these cold and empty London churches less than four out of every hundred West Indians go.

The churches have failed to hold these Christian immigrants not because their clergy and members have neglected,
repelled, or slighted the West Indians; on the contrary, they
have welcomed them to services, invited them to socials, visited them (when they can find them; immigrants move
around a lot and never leave addresses), and done their best
to carry out their Christian duties. There has been no colour
bar. They've failed because they have treated the immigrants
as they would treat their English fellows: they've been polite,
according to their lights friendly, and have respected the
newcomers' privacy.

To the English this respecting of privacy is the essence of
good manners; to the West Indians it is a form of brush-off, as
if a man stuffed his hands in his pockets when you held out
yours for a friendly shake. Again, a clash of customs, of ideas,
a failure to mesh. In respecting a desire for privacy we respect
something these others haven't got, don't want, and may believe to be a symptom of a sick mind.

When the shock wears off, most West Indians grow philosophic. "You stay like a bird in a tree not shaking your wings,
you get on fine." Again: "You don't want to shoot your
mouth off here." Or: "The English, they'll help you, but
they don't want to know you." The Nottingham sociologist
who elicited these remarks found that four out of every five
West Indians he questioned, after two years or more of life in
Britain, believed that they'd done right to come here and
would settle for good.

"There's good and bad in all countries. They treat me
right here. I don't complain." This was Fred, a Dominican
borough cleaner. He and his wife had a flat off the Portobello

Road with two rooms and its own cooker on the landing, and knew themselves lucky. In Dominica they'd owned a small banana patch but couldn't live on what it brought in. "Back home we have to pay for school and doctor, and if we can't pay we go without. But here you get sick, the doctor he come and don't want no money."

Fred was painting a door bright blue with slow, careful brushstrokes so as not to spill the paint. Was there anything he lacked here? He dipped his brush and laid on a few strokes, gently biting his tongue. "Someone to accept me."

His wife washed up most evenings at a hospital after the children were in bed. "They kindly," she said. "They don't treat me bad." Any real friends? She shook her head. In three years she had never been asked inside an English home. "All doors are open to West Indians," someone has observed, "except the ultimate door, the door of the English home." Mainly this is laziness; it applies also to Americans or Australians; and the English are far from unique. French homes are said to be even more impregnable. But Caribbeans either read into the situation a deliberate slight or else are wounded by indifference. So they turn in on themselves, which anyway requires less effort; they don't have to struggle to speak correct English, they can relapse into their own island dialect, laugh at the same jokes, turn the radio on at full blast and stamp and sing, recall familiar scenes and people.

"We are drifting into apartheid through mutual agreement," a rueful social worker said. While in theory this course is repugnant to both communities, in daily life both find it easier. "They're retreating into ghettos." It's true that whole streets are "going black" as the natives leave and coloured immigrants move in.

3

You can see this in Shepherd's Bush or Portobello Road, where to walk, or rather weave, a tortuous way between the barrows on a Saturday morning is like entering another world. Of course there *are* palefaces, but the main impression is of colour. Skins chocolate and toffee and polished mahogany, ochre and dun; saris and cloths, robes and berets and cardigans and head scarfs in garish hues. And purplish-pink sweet potatoes, green plantains, maroon eggplants, crinkled passion fruit.

An Indian woman with a square, nut-brown, kindly face sits at a stall spread with trinkets and tiny phials of Eastern perfumes, pungent and queer; she speaks no English, but her schoolboy son interprets; he is bright and eager; three and six a phial, he says. Every Saturday they sell twenty or thirty phials. Jamaicans barge along the pavement trailing shopping carts piled high with groceries and bargain fiercely for bits of yam; full of self-confidence, nearly all are fat, solid, and healthy, their purses stuffed, it seems, with currency.

A paunchy Jew tries to auction sheets and bedspreads; no one bids; a nun sidles up and buys a face towel for one and six. A Levantine—Syrian, Lebanese, Egyptian?—strides by, dressed like an English squire in a tweed jacket and a porkpie hat, smoking a pipe. A heavily pregnant Indian surges past him with her stomach thrust out proudly, like the blunt nose of a bulldozer. A Malayan type with slashed cheekbones inspects junk on a stall.

There's junk everywhere you wouldn't think existed: moulting top hats, jet-encrusted reticules, bits of fur tippet, writhing brass candlesticks, stall after stall of jewelry of a cheap-and-nastiness that staggers the eye. Barrow boys shout, exhort, bargain, wisecrack, shout again. A thin, grey-headed, desiccated man bends over an electric hand drill carefully cutting a key. A bedraggled Irishwoman with three skirt-clinging, dirt-smeared brats examines an old double bed with brass bedposts. (For the West African market these are made to rattle loudly when the bed's in use, signalling the owner's virility.) There are piles of old clothes. Baby carriages. Packed shops with Pakistani and Sikh names. "Fresh this morning"—dayshin, straight from Cyprus. "Yams today."

4

Integrationists of all races put their faith in the young, who won't be immigrants, but native-born. (And this is to be remembered when looking at the figures; children of immigrants born in Britain count, of course, as British, and yet generally belong to an immigrant community; it won't be long before you can double, and then double again, the numbers of West Indians or Asians in these islands officially listed as immigrants, if you want to arrive at the true size of the community.) And yet no one has succeeded in getting a racially mixed youth club off the ground.

Everyone concerned has tried hard. In Leeds a soft-voiced, gentle Trinidadian, just off duty from a night shift in a bus garage, told me of attempts going back ten years. After his discharge from the R.A.F. he took a job as cleaner for a Boys'

Brigade headquarters in London's East End. The boys grew more interested in petty larceny than in church parades, the club wilted, and the Trinidadian asked if he could try to revive it. He began to coach a few boys in cricket, hired some brass instruments, and started a band. The band caught on, the club formed a cricket eleven and never looked back.

These were white boys. When Mr. Edwards moved to Leeds, he nursed for years the notion of a mixed club, but no one had the money or, even more difficult, the premises. At last a dilapidated church hall was found; a public appeal raised the money, and now fifty or sixty teenagers gather there once a week. But gradually most of the white members have drifted away.

Mr. Edwards isn't despondent. "The day will come. Perhaps through cricket." An interest in cricket seems to be almost the only natural point of contact between hosts and immigrants. In public transport each garage is the busman's social unit, and has its club. Very few West Indians join these clubs. They're not kept out, they just don't come. "They seem to have no confidence." But for cricket they turn out in force. For a while one of the clubs had a mixed eleven. But it's not mixed any longer, it's all coloured. Racial friction? "No. They picked the best men, and all the best men were Caribbeans."

5

We live, in Britain, by a series of small, irrational, rigid, and unwritten laws. So, to some extent, do all societies, but our conventions are perhaps more numerous and complex than most. As with our language, you have to pick them up by usage as you go along. A stranger is like a fly blundering into an invisible web.

Of a number of examples here are two. A Jamaican busman walked into his canteen, thumped on the bar, and demanded, "Hey, there, bring a glass of water." The white barman glared. "What was that you said, mate?" "I said a glass of water, and make it snappy." The barman told the busman where to put the glass of water, and before long both men were at it hammer and tongs. The busman could have had his glass of water if he'd said that he needed an aspirin. For everything there's a technique. But if two men fall out over a glass of water and one is white and one is coloured, then it's a race riot—at any rate, if the press is anywhere around.

In the canteen of an old-established clothing factory in the North certain tables are reserved, by long tradition, for the cutters, who form a tight little aristocracy of their own. The sacredness of these tables is known, without a word being said, to all 6,000 employees of the firm, and had never been violated—until the West Indians came.

Two plump, flouncing young Jamaican girls dumped their plates at one of these tables, sat down brusquely, and talked in loud voices. The cutters ate in stunned silence, their eyes turned away. No one said anything the first day, hoping it would blow over. The second day the girls brought several friends. "If they'd been white girls," the personnel officer said, "the men would simply have told them to buzz off, and that would have been the end of it. As it was, for several days the men said nothing, and then one of them spoke up, politely but firmly, and said that the table had always been reserved for men."

There was a fine old rumpus. The girls raised the cry of "colour bar," marched out of the canteen, and complained to union and management. White men refusing to sit with coloured girls! The factory buzzed. Had the press got hold of it, there'd have been a headlined colour-bar story. In the end the management got one of the older West Indian women to soothe the girls' feelings and it died down. But the girls never were convinced that they hadn't been racially insulted.

"It's colour, colour, colour all the time, till I could scream," said a Birmingham welfare officer. "Chips as big as pine logs on their shoulders. You can't blame them, I know, but sometimes . . ."

This applies especially to Caribbeans. They come expecting the moon and get a lemon. They feel betrayed. It's irremediable, because often the betrayer isn't race prejudice, which we could remedy, but our national character, which (at least quickly) we can't.

6

Asian attitudes are much less complex. There's none of this love-hate, mother-son, betrayer-and-betrayed relationship. They have never shared our culture and don't intend to, having one of their own with which they're perfectly satisfied. They come in search of economic opportunity, not social acceptance. Here are no emotional undertones.

As they come expecting less, most of them are the less disillusioned. The conditions we find so distressing, overcrowding and unsanitary living, are, to a majority, superior to anything they have known before. Probably a million people sleep out every night in the streets in Calcutta because they've nowhere else to go. Here at least they have walls, roofs, and beds, however squalid these are. The education of their children, if they bring any, the medical attention they receive, are privileges few have even imagined. Such disappointments as they have relate almost solely to money; imagining good jobs to grow on trees like mangoes, if they find themselves on national assistance they come down to earth with a bump.

Safely buttoned up in their communities, Asians do not normally look out for insults or fly off the handle, as a rule, if these occur. When a smallpox epidemic was started by immigrants from Pakistan and the small boys of Bradford jeered and called it "pakipox," they didn't retaliate. (Though there was a hefty Indian who, insulted by the word "blackie," kept an English workmate up a crane all through the lunch hour by standing at its foot in an attitude of menace.) They don't frequent coffee bars to look for girls. Their general attitude is negative and self-effacing. So, on the whole, they present a problem mainly to local authorities, because of housing, health, and education, and to those who believe in integration so strongly that they want to see it brought about even when the immigrants don't.

But, of course, Asians have their feelings and are not fools. "Pakistanis are proud," one of their number said. "We conquered India. We are accustomed to look down on others, not to be looked down on, as some of the British do. That's why we are reserved." He qualified this by saying that he meant West Pakistanis, from the Punjab; Bengalis from East Pakistan he dismissed with contempt. "Many are untouchables who turned Muslim to escape their status."

He added, "We think this about the British: whatever their personal feelings may be, they'll give you your rights. An Englishman may hate your guts, but he'll give you your place in the queue. The English are stiff, reserved, and sometimes lack human feeling; there's no warmth; the women domineer; but they are a mature people. There's a sense of stability. They have taken advantage of their past."

Two aspects of British life really shocked him; the disrespect and sometimes insolence of the young towards their parents—"I should have died of shame if I had spoken thus before my father"—and, even more, neglect of the old. He could scarcely believe that any old person with a single living relative could be put into an institution.

"To us that is unthinkable. Our religion forbids it. There is no old-age problem in Islam. We have a saying: 'Paradise lies under the feet of the mother.' No salvation would be possible for anyone who neglected her. In our family we are three brothers, and we compete to have our mother with us; she is old and sick, and we retain the best doctors in Karachi to visit her every day."

Come to that, there's the Fifth Commandment; and a Caribbean calypso:

> *I can always get another wife,*
> *But I can never get another mother in my life.*

14. Students

NORMALLY students aren't immigrants, so don't really belong here. But some who come to study stay for good, and others may arrive with that concealed intention. The number of students, like practically everything else, is proliferating. Our universities, technical colleges, teacher training colleges, hospitals, and other institutions where higher education and professional and commercial training are purveyed today offer places to more than five times as many overseas students as they did in 1950. (Then, rather over 12,000; now, just under 65,000.)

These are full-time, properly accredited students, here for over six months, in pursuit of recognized diplomas or degrees: the real McCoy. There is, in addition, a fringe world of pupils at evening classes who are wage earners by day; others involved with dubious, even bogus, institutions; people who come for three months and stay for years; many other kinds. There's no way to keep track of these; if all were counted, the roll of students would be at least doubled.

Roughly two out of every three of the officially listed 65,000 come from Commonwealth countries; of these Nigeria sends by far the largest number—about 9,000, or nearly one in four. India and Jamaica all but tie for second place, still a long way behind Nigeria, with Malaysia third, followed by Ghana and Trinidad. At the foot of the list come Samoa, the Falkland Islands, and the New Hebrides, each sending three or under. Counting these tiny satellites, students converge here from forty-six fragments of the Commonwealth. (And from ninety-six foreign lands, including Qatar, Curaçao and Dubai—plus Ireland, still neither Commonwealth nor foreign.)

More than half converge on London. A few years ago a majority would have been in the universities, teacher training colleges or Inns of Court, in line for desk, dais and white collar, or wig; now many more are in pursuit of technical skills than of intellectual attainments. When it comes to the two cultures, and leaving on one side medicine and, the largest category of all, those merely trying to get their General Certificate of Education, about twice as many overseas students go in for science and technology as for the arts and social studies. This reflects an awakening in their homelands to the urgent need to leave behind an almost total dependence on peasant farming and find employment for their ever mounting millions of school-leavers who seek a livelihood without a hoe in their hands.

2

Roughly one student out of every ten in Britain is a nonnative. (There should be a word for nonnatives: overseasmen? Transoceaners?) In London University this proportion rises to one quarter (6,600 overseasmen in a total muster of 26,-700), in some provincial universities it falls to one in twenty or so. Accommodation is the headache. And, once again, nonnatives share this headache with the natives, but exacerbate it both by swelling numbers and by lacking other resources. A fair proportion of British students either live at home or find quarters with friends or relatives; this overseasmen can't do. Most of them fall back on landladies.

Until a few years ago the landlady was a daunting figure, slamming her door in the faces of many coloured students and overcharging the rest. There's still plenty of colour prejudice, of course; but more landladies take in coloured students than debar them, and to find a notice in a shop window, these days, saying Regret No Coloured would require a diligent search. Perhaps this is merely because most landladies have learned more tactful ways of turning coloured people from their doors. But while every coloured student will tell you that discrimination is rife, it's surprising how few can give you a convincing personal example. Like ghost stories, many of the experiences turn out to have befallen a friend of a friend.

To many overseas students the British Council now plays the part of universal aunt. Its emissaries meet the newcomers at dock or airport and take them in charge from the moment they set foot on British concrete. The Council's officers believe their moment of acceptance came when students willingly surrendered their hand baggage, provided that a British Council man took charge of it.

"If you'd come from Timbuktu or Tonga," one of them said, "with everything you possess in a suitcase, and fetched up in a completely strange land, wouldn't you cling on to your bag? It not only contains all your possessions, it's your

symbol of home, your link with the familiar—a fragment of
your native land. Would *you* give it up to a total stranger?
How would you know you'd ever see it again? For years they
wouldn't do it, but now the word's gone around—trust the
British Council and you'll get it back. So it's a point of hon-
our with us that every student must be reunited with his
luggage the same evening he arrives. We pride ourselves
we've never yet failed, though it's been a near thing at
times."

At the splendid new students' centre in Portland Place,
run by the Council—a hub of overseasman life—there's a sort
of operations room where the meeting, transportation, sort-
ing out, and placing of the visitors are organized. There's a
staff of couriers permanently on duty to meet almost every
flight at London Airport and almost every boat train at the
London termini. In theory, the Council is warned in advance
by the airline, by the government of the student's country, or
by its own man on the spot; in practice, airlines, students,
and governments are wayward, and totally unheralded flights
quite often arrive. Not long ago a batch of students from
Brunei reached Luton without any previous warning. To
meet such situations the couriers have developed a sort of
sixth sense, or perhaps it is a network of spies; somehow they
learned about the Luton arrivals and met them in the middle
of the night.

Almost without exception, students are sponsored by some
body, institution, or department which, on its side, considers
its responsibilities more or less discharged when its protégés
board the vessel or aircraft headed for Britain. But few of the
students have any idea what to do when they arrive. The
Council's arrangements to meet, shepherd, and convey them
to their places of study form a lifeline indeed. Before it was

proffered, Communist agents were said to fish many of these floundering students out of the sea. They would have to move smartly, these days, to carry out this rescue work, and it is unlikely that any student would surrender his bulging suitcase, stuffed perhaps with a few parting kola nuts or yams, to the most persuasive comrade if he could see a British Council courier around. Here is the Council's score for a single day in September 1963, chosen at random: twenty flights met, plus seven ships and eight boat trains; 295 new arrivals from thirty-one countries; baggage handled, 733 pieces. Everyone got his suitcase, a bed for the night, and within a few days, accommodation at his place of study.

3

At Portland Place there's a register of lodgings with a code of symbols to indicate the preferences of every individual landlady. Here, in confidence, she can impose a private colour bar, or the reverse. Some take in browns but not blacks; some prefer blacks to whites; some ask for Canadians rather than Latin Americans, or vice versa; some break down the different kinds of coloured and will take Barbadians but not Jamaicans, or Sikhs but not Muslims, or Caribbeans but not Africans, or Malays but not Greeks. Almost everyone likes the Chinese.

What determines these tastes? "Experience. If a student's a success, the landlady wants another like him. If he's not, she'll tar them all with the same brush." Which is commoner, to dislike or like your lodger? "More successes than failures,

far more." But the great problem is to find enough landladies. The shortage is acute. Taking in lodgers doesn't pay,
or it pays very poorly; it's too much trouble; people are moving out of the centres of big cities and into smaller houses or
flats; and nowadays most women prefer to earn their money
by going out to work.

The answer lies in hostels and halls of residence; everyone
knows this; it's a question of money. Halls and hostels are
going up, but no one can keep pace with the big increase in
the number of college students. The government's recent
three-million-pound grant to help build, adapt, and equip
hostels for overseas students is a beginning, but there's a long
way to go; at present only one student in seven or eight gets a
chance to live in a hostel.

For the lodgers loneliness is the bugbear. "The English
students speak to us after lectures; they're polite, but they
don't make friends with us, they never ask us to their homes."
This was from an African in Nottingham, but it might have
been any overseasman anywhere. Two Guianan girls who
shared accommodation added, "When we come home to our
room, we talk only to each other. We've made no friends."

What about all the university activities—Student Union
dances, film shows, the 101 clubs and societies that cater to
special interests? Most of the students looked blank. "We're
not invited." You don't have to be invited, I pointed out;
you just go. "We've no friends to go with."

Are they shy, or is the trouble, once again, a difference in
outlook and custom? In their own countries perhaps they'd
have been formally invited; here they waited for an invitation that never came. And few seemed to have any interests
outside their work. An exception was a Tanganyikan who'd
enrolled in a course for football referees; and he seemed to be

the happiest. This narrowness of outlook is typical, under-standable but inhibiting. An African student asked around to coffee looked at his host's bookshelves. "I thought you were a professor of agriculture." "Yes, I am." "Then what are these books on Greece doing here?"

In hostels overseasmen are able to venture from their na-tional and racial shells. "I never made an English friend until I came here," said a Ugandan in Birmingham. "Now I think they're human after all." There aren't many rules in this hostel, but two at least are strictly enforced: about one in-mate in four must be English; and pairs who share rooms must hail from different countries.

It was an English boy who was strumming a guitar after coffee, singing hillbilly songs. Africans got their legs pulled when they started talking politics, as Africans always do. "I wouldn't have missed this for anything," an English boy said. "It's opened up whole new worlds. They're so *alive*. And now I'll have friends in half a dozen different countries if I go abroad later on." Every place in this and every other hostel is heavily oversubscribed.

4

Many overseasmen are old, for students; some are married, and bring their wives. Then, generally, they bring trouble: accommodation, again, and money. A scholarship or grant ample for one, by local standards, spells penury for two or more in Britain. Some turn themselves into wage earners by day and study by night. Quite often their money runs out.

"I've been here seven years," said a Nigerian I spoke to in his good, clean bed-sitting room—no hugger-muggering for him—off the King's Road. "After three years my father died, and I had no money. Now I'm a charge hand in an engineering works. The pay's good, I like the work, and at night I study." Piles of textbooks on the table proved his words. When did he expect to get his degree? "Another two or three years . . ." Nigerians are in no hurry. Many seem perfectly happy to stay eight or ten years, confident that in the end they'll go back to a good job and a welcoming family. (Maybe too welcoming; it's said that some students stay on here to dodge their demands.)

Far from having trouble over rooms and landladies, this Nigerian left his previous quarters because he was *too* happy —overintegrated. "I was one of the family. The landlady was a mother to me. She kept my clothes and did my washing and looked after my health. She has a daughter who is like my sister. I can go there anytime I like, drop in, there's always a welcome for me." Then why . . .? "I felt I was becoming English, ceasing to be African—I was losing my Nigerian personality."

Here he touched upon a major difference between Africans and West Indians. (There are far more differences than similarities; pigment, in fact, is almost the only characteristic common to both.) West Indians want to integrate, Africans don't. Another student said, "In London we Nigerians don't live as a community because we don't need to; we have an old culture, as you have, so we don't feel inferior. As for the West Indians, they've no culture of their own, so they must borrow yours, but it's secondhand—like picking up discarded cigarette ends." There was no mistaking the edge of contempt in his voice.

After six years of rather desultory study this Nigerian had just been called to the Bar; grave, unflurried, bearded, mature, articulate, speaking English more fluently than most English people, and seeming already to be spiritually clothed in judicial wig and robes, he'd employed his time not merely in learning his craft but in gaining experience. He'd travelled on the Continent, made English friends, read books, seen plays, listened to music. "But I prefer our own. Your music is too different, it speaks to the intellect and not the heart." Any difficulties, troubles, colour bar? He shook his head. "It's there, of course, you can feel it, but I haven't come up against any personal experiences—probably because I've taken care to avoid situations where it might arise."

His Nigerian culture—what did it consist of, how did he pursue it here in his Bayswater room? A blue-and-white-striped cotton robe hung on the door. "In the evenings I often change into cloth and sandals; but that's nothing. How can one explain a culture? It's an outlook, the shape of one's mind. You pick up a shell on the beach. Inside there's been an animal, and all animals are made of the same chemicals, but each kind makes a different shape of shell . . ." Now he's married a Nigerian midwife and is going home to a waiting job, while his bride stays behind to complete her training.

Had I been a Nigerian, he'd have offered me a kola nut, symbol of hospitality among his people. "Like your English cup of tea," he said. Nearby, the Shepherd's Bush market has a shop devoted wholly to West African foods with enticing names like gbure and okra, tete and apan, obelawo and egusi, garden eggs and fou-fou, edwene and dried snails. Here hefty, buxom ladies wrapped in gorgeous technicolour robes with hair either de-kinked and wound in high, coal-scuttle-like cones, or done in tight curls all over, jostle and stretch, pick and choose and bargain to fill their baskets with food freshly come by air. They glisten with health, abound with vitality, ooze self-confidence; there's nothing about them diffident, uncertain, or shy. In the estimation of West Indians these Africans are rich, snobbish, arrogant, standoffish, and proud, despising anyone who has the misfortune not to be an African. Theirs is the earth and everything that's in it, and they're not inclined to share it with anyone else—certainly not with a working-class Caribbean.

5

Not all Africans in Britain, of course, are students, though these—counting in the demi-students—may well be in a majority. No one knows how many African nonstudents there are; perhaps about 30,000, mainly West Africans, with a sprinkling from the East and Centre, plus a small but growing contingent of Somalis.

By and large, they spurn the lowlier occupations; you seldom find them cleaning streets, conducting buses, wheeling gravel, collecting litter. A railway porter with whom I got into conversation turned out to be a chief's son from Kenya, but he was a university student doing a vacation job. Like American soldiers in World War II, a surprising number of whom claimed ownership of Texas ranches, Africans are very apt to be princes, sons of chiefs, or heirs to emirates; their lively imaginations, respect for hierarchy, and talent for myth-making unite to romanticize and inflate their personalities.

"Intelligent but difficult" was the way West Africans were

summed up by a social worker who comes into contact with a good many. "They're touchy, and inclined to lack a sense of humour; independent; they sort out their own problems more than other immigrants. Go their own ways. Some are in the vice racket. West Africans own most of the brothels in this town."

"They live off white girls," is a stereotyped charge against Africans, like the Caribbeans' Kit-e-Kat sandwiches; there's no way of measuring its truth or falsity. Perhaps envy is a hidden source of the charge. Growing Indian hemp in back gardens is another activity of which they're sometimes accused. There's no way of knowing whether the proportion of offenders is higher among Africans than it is amongst the natives, or any other group of immigrants.

Most African nonstudents, of course, are usefully and respectably employed. There's a growing number of doctors. I spoke to an education officer whose committee had gone to some trouble to engage several West African teachers. Their idea was to implant in the minds of English children the image of the coloured man as an authority, a superior, in place of the more usual one of social inferiority.

"They were well liked as individuals," he said of the West Africans, "but their teaching methods were very old-fashioned." In what way? "Too dictatorial." In the schools run by this authority, knowledge was imparted by guidance and encouragement rather than by direct instruction; no child held up a hand if he wanted to leave the classroom, he simply wandered out and came back when he felt inclined. This horrified the African teachers, trained in a more orthodox school.

"Besides, in the canteen one of them—a woman—spat her peach stones out onto the floor . . . On the whole, the experiment was a failure." A school in another area, however, had on its staff a Trinidadian, a Sikh, and a Pakistani, all reported successes. As with lodgers, there are more successes than failures.

6

Next to Nigeria, more students come from India than from any other Commonwealth country. (Iraq sends the largest contingent of foreigners; then—a tie—France and Germany.) Just as in Nigeria "been-to's" enjoy a social *cachet* denied to stay-at-homes, so does a British diploma or degree confer upon Indians social prestige as well as a professional stamp. So it is worth pledging every resource and pulling every string to get to Britain; but when they do, many Indian students are disappointed.

Our cities are dirtier, our streets drabber, our manners ruder than they expected; above all, our people are more unfriendly. To some all this is positively alarming. A survey carried out for Political and Economic Planning in 1961 by Mr. A. K. Singh (*Indian University Students in Britain*) reports how, in an old house, "an old landlady loitered round the whole day with a dog in her lap and stared at me with the frightening, empty look of a dying person. She'd hung a placard on the wall which read, 'Dog is a better friend than man.'" No wonder the student "left the ghostly atmosphere after a week."

Then there's colour prejudice. Asked by Mr. Singh whether this existed, 72 percent said "Yes," but only 37 per-

cent could produce a personal experience. Least discrimination was reported from Oxford and Cambridge, most from
London. And sometimes well-meaning efforts by the natives
misfired. An Indian invited to a party where he found a
Nigerian and a West Indian also at his host's table felt that
he'd been paraded as a specimen—as if his host had rung up
the British Council and ordered "one of each."

There are sex problems, too. News, it seems, has spread in
India of the free-and-easiness of European girls, and students
come with great expectations, only to find themselves
trapped by unscrupulous doxies or mortally offending respectable young ladies. Separation from their wives naturally
distresses married students, who are many, and generally
harassed by having to support a family at home. And married
Indian men are fantastically pampered. "I had got used to a
life," one confessed, "in which every morning I found the
bath ready, blade put into the safety razor, fresh clothes on
the hangers, and breakfast on the table. Now I have to do
everything myself, and I cannot do them properly. My landlady always complains . . ."

Academically many find themselves less well equipped
than they had supposed and their English inadequate. This
means extra work, and sometimes disaster. "For two years I
have lost my salary in India and spent my own money here.
Now I have no savings, my wife has no ornaments, and I am
heavily in debt. I have earned only humiliations. I do not
know what I should do."

It is always surprising to see ourselves through other
people's eyes. Apparently, in Indian opinion, we excel in
Roman virtues and lack most of the humane ones. Mr. Singh
went around asking Indian students to grade us by qualities.
For being "honest," "responsible," "disciplined," and "hard-

working" we scored well over 90 percent. (For "disciplined"
—those bus queues!—98 percent, against a score of only 6
percent awarded by the Indians to themselves.) For being
"active" we scored 86 percent, and Indians only 9. Our score
for being "strong" was 84 percent, Indians' 10.

But when it came to personal and domestic virtues, the
situation was reversed. Indians scored over 90 percent for
being "affectionate," "kind," "cordial," "informal," and
"hospitable." We were badly down on all those—right down
to 4 percent for informality; 31 percent for being "cordial,"
38 percent for "affectionate," and 41 percent for "kind."
While those students who were questioned felt saddened and
rebuffed by our lack of affection, hospitality, and kindness,
they appreciated our relative efficiency.

"Here, in the libraries, they help you to find the book; if
it's not available, they borrow it from another library or purchase it for you; in India you just have to come back, and if
the book isn't on the shelves forget about it. Here they trust
you; you get your cheque cashed at the counter; in India you
have to wait for hours to draw your money." Another student
said he liked our public speeches because they began on time
and ended promptly, whereas in India the speaker often arrived an hour late, another hour was spent in garlanding him
with flowers and paying equally flowery compliments, and
then he held forth, "mostly without notes or relevance, until
he had exhausted himself and the audience."

Our hospitality, when extended, they tended to find grudg-
ing and glum. "They invite you a month in advance, remind
you of the date, and send a diagram explaining the way; after
all this they will serve you with boiled potatoes and roast
lamb! They even expect you to travel a long way just for a
cup of coffee or a sip of sherry."

Our treatment of the elderly shocked them, and so did our lack of religious faith. Nevertheless, the great majority were glad they'd come. They believed they had acquired experience, balance, and a closer understanding of the West—and of their own culture, too. While they saw, by comparison with Western standards, how poor and backward was their own society, they did not want to change its cultural values, its heart and soul. These they cherished all the more for their glimpse of another set of cultural ideas. They went home resolved to keep India Indian, but to bring it technologically up to date.

7

What, exactly, *is* a student? The word can be stretched to include almost anyone. Some say it is, indeed, being so stretched, to cover those who wish to bypass the Commonwealth Immigrants Act. Proof of this is naturally hard to find.

Take beauty culture and hairdressing, perfectly legitimate skills with two or three years' apprenticeship. An advertisement:

> DAME X'S INSTITUTE OF BEAUTY CULTURE:
> Lectures in Anatomy, Electricity
> Physiology, Chemistry, Physiotherapy

A photograph depicts Dame X surrounded by a bevy of dusky graduates in caps and gowns, clasping diplomas and bouquets, with a West African prince in the middle and an address in London's East End.

Dame X was unfortunately out at the time of my visit; her Institute consisted of an upstairs salon with three or four hair-washing basins and a small basement room. Here a couple of African ladies were chatting while a pleasant young Jamaican girl combed the hair of one of them. Furnishings consisted of a few chairs, a couple of mirrors, photographs of hair styles on damp-stained walls, and a playful kitten.

What about lectures? The Jamaican looked vague. "Mrs. X, she give them sometimes, Wednesday and Saturdays." Chemistry, electricity, physiology? "Maybe." Many students? "Oh yes, plenty come." What do they pay? "She never say." Any outside lecturers? The assistant shook her head. The Institute appeared to be a one-man band.

Then there's hairdressing. A report in a daily newspaper: "Nigerians posing as students of hairdressing are using a loophole in the Commonwealth Immigrants Act to enter Britain. When accepted by schools in this country, they are given a passport by the Nigerian emigration authorities and allowed to enter Britain, but they fail to enroll or to pay any fees."

There's little doubt that a racket, profitable to both sides, has sprung up. Two respectable ladies in the West of England run, or ran, an establishment to teach English to foreigners and initiate them into English life—cathedrals, Shakespeare at Stratford, museums, art galleries: a useful all-round course for young Europeans.

Why only Europeans? The coloured young need these facilities just as much, and the two ladies decided to help cement the bonds of Commonwealth by inviting them in. An advertisement inserted into several Nigerian newspapers had a startling result: nine hundred applications poured in. The ladies raised a mortgage to buy another house, enlarged their own, and installed an up-to-date system of central heating. Then they wrote to accept ninety of the applicants, laid in equipment and supplies, engaged daily workers, received enthusiastic replies from the chosen Nigerians, and prepared for the big day.

The day came; they met the train from London; not a single Nigerian arrived. Nor did they come the next day, nor the day after . . . About thirty subsequently wrote from different parts of Britain to say that they had changed their minds; from the other sixty, no word. On the strength of their letters of acceptance the Nigerians had been able to claim passports and to enter Britain as bona fide students, untrammelled by the red tape attached to vouchers, acts of Parliament, and other tiresome bureaucratic controls. Then they had found the jobs they had always intended to take.

15. Some Conclusions

"Do ENGLISHWOMEN ever buy yams?" "Now and then," said the barrow owner. He served a customer and thought again. "Well, not really. Not what we're used to, are they?"

Extract from a report on Pakistanis in Bradford: "B is a married man living with his wife and family in a Council house amongst English neighbours. He speaks little English, but his job fits his capabilities and his sons are doing well at school. His wife has incorporated queen cakes and Yorkshire pudding into her menus."

The window of an Indian photographer in Leeds. Every picture shows a wedding group of Caribbeans. White, lace-covered dresses, trains at least twelve feet long, eight or ten bridesmaids. The groom stands stiffly at attention in his dark suit and white carnation and gloves, throwing out his chest. Wedding guests cluster around with ornate hats and bouquets, tight suits, and shining shoes. In the background is a grime-encrusted red brick church or chapel.

Once a couple gets well established here, they start to think about a wedding. It confers prestige. The children they've left behind, the old folks, and a whole bevy of relations will finger the pictures with pride, joy, and deep respect. Nathaniel and Rebecca surely prosper, they can afford a church wedding like that. A status symbol—no doubt a legacy of the past when slaves couldn't marry, only the free. (That went on till 1830.)

In Jamaica four children in five are born out of wedlock. In London, among Jamaicans, this falls to one in four. (The London average is one in seven.) The English marry and expect others to. "We want to live like you," say Caribbeans. The British don't follow the Caribbean example; the Caribbeans follow ours. They take to Yorkshire pudding, not we to yams.

So far we've started on the process of digesting our minorities not without hiccoughs and rumbles, but with no major upset. Will this continue? Is there a limit to our digestive capacity? If so, where and how is it to be set? What is the ultimate aim? Integration? Total assimilation? Or some form of apartheid by mutual consent? Are we, by not taking foresight, creating problems we may find ourselves unable to solve?

Public opinion seems to be about as clear as it ever is in our compromising, halfway-house, issue-evading country. Immigration is like a wet day. We don't really *want* it to happen, but know it's good for the gardens, and anyway, we can't stop it, so might as well make the best of things. And once we've got it, we must be fair. The newcomers must be treated decently: no incipient ghettos, segregation, colour bar—in theory at least.

There are, of course, dissidents, ranging from neo-fascists who go about chalking Keep Britain White on walls to the landlady who has nothing *against* the coloured people but would rather not have one in the house. They are in a minority, but a substantial minority, and one that could grow. While race discrimination is out of fashion nowadays, quite a number of citizens harbour doubts, fears, and resentments that they are, in the present climate of opinion, ashamed to admit. And one must remember that revealing survey of schoolchildren's attitudes. In a school without a single coloured pupil not a single white one expressed race prejudice; in a school heavily loaded with foreigners and coloured 85 percent did.

2

Integration is the key word. The Shorter Oxford Dictionary defines this as "The making up of a whole by adding together or combining the separate parts or elements; a making whole or entire." We must combine dark-skinned West Indians and Africans and Asians, not to mention all the paler, but no less alien, Poles and Italians and Cypriots and Hungarians and Jews and Ukranians and Maltese and Arabs into one entire nation.

Or perhaps the verb *assimilate* comes nearer to our true meaning? "To cause to resemble; to make alike." Those immigrants who settle here, we consider, should come to resemble us and be made alike: digested, melted down. Become responsible Britishers; get married, eat Yorkshire pudding, speak English, keep their children clean and their appointments punctually, wear proper clothes, join trade unions, use the lavatory, mow the lawn, and respect their neighbours' privacy. Sooner or later, runs this train of thought, they must give up yams, girls' muslin trousers, jabbering in foreign tongues, unsanitary habits, noisy parties, hugger-muggering in dormitories, leaving the garbage about, spreading small-pox, tuberculosis, and V.D., having too many babies, and generally being un-British, as we think. Become like us: assimilated.

How far do we, and they, really want this to go? All the way? Or should there be, and could there be, a halfway house in which any community that so wished could keep its own customs while sharing our lives—a sort of semi-detached halfway house? As, for example, French Canadians seem to occupy in Quebec?

Opinions vary. At one end of the scale many people think that immigrants—a word they're inclined to equate with coloured—should be treated as equals at work and in the social services, but that in private life we and they are, on the whole, better apart. They'd make no hard and fast rules about this, and indeed, make plenty of exceptions when it comes to coloured immigrants who are "better educated"—in other words, middle class. They willingly accept, for instance, Asian doctors. A Jamaican parson in a white working-class district in the North told me he'd not experienced a single instance of rejection or hostility because of his colour—not just among his flock, but among the general run of citizens. Like their employers, most people "look to the man and not the colour" in situations like these.

It's intermarriage that really sticks in the gills. "Would you like *your* daughter to marry a Negro?" Either we must return a forthright "Yes" or—and this is far more likely—a reluctant "Not *like* it, but it's got to come, and the boy and girl must decide for themselves." Acceptance, whether we assimilate or integrate.

It takes, however, two to make a mixed marriage. "What would you do if your daughter went out with an English boy?" This question was put to a Sikh in Southall. "She'd be back in the Punjab within a week." To him, and to all his fellows, the very thought of intermarriage was repugnant. The great majority of mixed marriages take place between coloured men and white girls. This Sikh would mind, but mind rather less, if his son were to walk out with an English-woman. It is the woman's place to conform, be moulded and assimilated; her children would become Sikhs. A daughter goes to the aliens and is lost.

Despite all this intermarriage must increase. So either we must bow to the inevitable or join the neo-fascists and campaign to "keep Britain white"—a lost cause anyway, because, counting in the natural increase, there must be a million coloured folk here already, and many more on the way. How many more? That brings us to the Commonwealth Immigrants Act.

3

Most people on the idealistic wing of our society opposed this act on grounds of principle. Our long tradition of free entry by any citizen of the Commonwealth must not (they said) be broken; we are the heart and centre of the Commonwealth, and must not deny to anyone its open shores. Here crops up, again, the image of the mother who has sent forth her sons and mustn't slam the door in the face of any who want to come home.

This is, alas, at bottom an imperialist, paternalistic notion, and it's ironical that the most anti-imperialist of our thinkers should be the ones to voice it most emphatically. Broken and tarnished lies the mother image; Asians and Africans never were her sons, anyway; her dugs are dry.

What is the Commonwealth, held up to the raw light of day? An idea in minds that, like all human minds, recoil from uncongenial reality, such as the loss of power and glory, and want to go on believing that as things were, so they remain. A sort of mummy case in which we have embalmed an empire that's dead but that we can't bring ourselves finally to bury because we want to go on feeling that something's still there. The Emperor's clothes.

Nor is the principle of free entry observed by any of the other members of the Commonwealth, or by any other major country in the world. No British citizen can enter as he pleases into Ghana or Uganda, India or Malaysia, Nigeria or Canada. The absolute necessity to control immigration is one of many fundamental, enormous, and as yet scarcely realized consequences of the population explosion. These consequences are going to change every aspect of human life on this planet—intellectual, spiritual, and social, as well as economic and material. So far it is only the material aspects to which we have given a little anxious thought—how we are to feed ourselves and build enough houses, schools, and roads. The spiritual and intellectual effects will be much more far-reaching and profound.

We can't, to begin with, go on pretending that a small island which already holds over fifty-two million people and is bursting at the seams can take in all who want to come, in unlimited numbers, from various parts of a commonwealth in which some 750 million people live and multiply, at a rate which is in itself increasing, by almost twenty million a year.

The number of Indians who will be born this year is larger than the whole population of Greater London; the next five years' annual increase would about double the population of the whole of Britain. Any suggestion that we might help them by acting as a safety valve for surplus people, with their awful problems of overpopulation, starvation, unemployment, and want, is merely ridiculous. These problems are beyond our power to alleviate in this way.

The whole business has become inextricably entangled with colour. It was because the act looked like a discriminatory act against coloured people that it was hated here. Many coloured people also thought it was an anti-coloured act. Basically—even with the Irish left out—it was not. The colour question was an enormous red herring—black herring, possibly—dragged across the path. It stank, and away went all the dedicated idealists in full pursuit.

But it *was* a herring, as many of the hounds are now prepared (at least in private) to admit. The real issue was a simple one: how many immigrants (black, brown, white, or yellow) can we in these islands, however much we may need their labour, provide with jobs, houses or rooms, transport, places in schools for their children, and hospital beds?

Obviously there's a practical answer. It can't be a million a year and it can't be none. Somewhere between the two lies an answer. As we don't plan, we have to guess. In 1963 those who came here from Commonwealth countries exceeded those who left by about 66,000. In addition about 16,000 aliens came to stay—a total of 82,000 newcomers, not counting the Irish. In 1964 the number was probably considerably larger. The joker in the pack is the number of dependents of those already here who, as we know, can enter without restriction.

4

Sandwiched between the nether taxpayers and the upper pol-
icy-makers in Westminster and Whitehall lies a whole layer
of unobtrusive persons, who occupy a sort of noncommissioned rank in our social hierarchy. These are local government officials and junior civil servants in the Ministries that
touch most closely on our social lives: housing managers and
education officers, public health inspectors and welfare ex-
perts, schoolteachers and probation officers, health visitors,
public transport managers, and the like. Faceless individuals,
they get on with their jobs and keep out of the limelight.
They have taken the brunt of the invasion, and their attitude
has, I think, been the unacknowledged but decisive factor in
shaping our national response. Like a cloud forming in the
sky, or like a tide exerting its invisible suction, their leadership, their pressure, has been exercised and applied to one
consistent direction: towards helping, accepting, and eventually assimilating the newcomers.

The housing manager said to me, "This is a crisis. My
whole policy will collapse if we give way." There were tears
in his eyes. The Council stood firm, and the strike collapsed.
This was a rent strike among white tenants who objected to
the allocation of a house to a coloured family on a new Council estate. The housing manager's policy was to ignore completely, in his system of priorities, any aspect of race.

A circular letter from a junior school headmaster to all
English parents: "Our last cleanliness inspection, carried out

yesterday, resulted in eight pupils being excluded from school—one immigrant child and seven English children. Our Grammar awards over the last ten years have averaged one in five of our school-leavers, and this average has been maintained since the arrival of our immigrant children."

Or from a factory manager: "To start with, we had trouble over the canteen—immigrants bringing their own food, and so on. With the co-operation of the union and the shop stewards, we invited the High Commission to send a man from London to give a talk about their homes and backgrounds. It went off well, and after that everything died down."

"We're trying to build up a civic consciousness among the immigrants. We've issued pamphlets in seven languages . . ." "We run a voluntary panel to investigate causes of friction between coloured and white neighbours—we try to meet trouble before it gets even halfway . . ." "A petition against a coloured family being given a Council house at Hitchin, Hertfordshire, was ignored by the Urban Council on a unanimous vote." Such instances can be multiplied indefinitely and found in almost every borough, county, and town hall. This unsung leadership has never been more solid, united, and consistent than it has been, on this issue, in the last few years.

Of course there have been exceptions. But, over the country as a whole, those in closest touch with the ordinary people in their homes and schools, their neighbourhoods and daily work, sickness and health—these paid officials, while they are the servants of the public, have in this case unobtrusively acted as its masters. They have told it there must be no colour bar in the allocation of housing, in schools, in hospitals, in public places. "I'm proud of my city," said a man who deals with immigrants in Birmingham, where tens of thousands have been taken in without any overt trouble, and with a great deal of goodwill.

These noncommissioned officers have been consistently backed up by those higher in the chain of command. "A form of apartheid in a public place in this country is revolting and repulsive," thundered a London magistrate, dismissing charges against demonstrators outside a pub said to segregate its coloured customers. Mayors have opened funds, Members of Parliament spoken passionately of the rights of man and the evils of prejudice, parsons not only preached but practiced brotherly love, and voluntary social workers toiled with devotion, single-mindedness, and competence to find practical ways in which people can integrate: halls they can meet in, places for youth clubs to gather, concerts to raise money, mixed sports teams, international friendship weeks, English tuition, evening classes for immigrants, weekend excursions, tea parties, receptions, panels of baby-sitters for working mothers—there's an endless list of down-to-earth and often boring things people of goodwill are performing all over the country, day after day. Councils of Social Service have brought together all these do-gooders, and they are doing good. But the leadership of these lieutenants and captains, firm as it has been, would not have made so strong an impact without the solidarity of the N.C.O.s in the town hall.

5

Can any general conclusion be extracted from this brief enquiry? The ease of integration varies inversely with the number of immigrants. And in every situation there is a threshold of safety. On one side lies a relatively smooth process of absorption, on the other the danger of open conflict between immigrant and host. Where that threshold lies must vary with circumstance, but it's nearly always there, and should be demarcated. Only the most doctrinaire would oppose demarcation on the grounds that there should not be any threshold at all; eating people is wrong, therefore there are no cannibals.

Changing the metaphor, one might use the analogy of a blood transfusion. Each human body can take so much of someone else's blood and no more. If you overdo the transfusion, and the patient's body cannot absorb so much alien blood so quickly, reactions are set up which can, and do, prove fatal. On the other hand, the same quantity dripped in gradually will strengthen the patient. It is the same with host and immigrants.

In schools and universities, in factories and public services, a ratio of immigrants to British—which generally means of coloured folk to whites—is often unofficially observed. In schools the threshold is widely considered to be somewhere between one quarter and one third immigrant. Some schools, as we have seen, have a roll two thirds immigrant or even higher. And here the lamb whose flag proclaims integration finds himself, strangely, lying down with the lion who roars apartheid. Too many immigrants don't integrate, they "clot," and set up, of their own volition, their own communities, quarters, and ghettos. So immigrant-lovers and immigrant-haters unite in wishing to see the proportion of newcomers kept down to a manageable level.

If there is one certain thing it is that the number of coloured children must rise, and continue to rise, for many years to come, in our schools. In some areas it will be hard, perhaps impossible, to keep on the right side of the threshold. Insofar as this depends on housing, there seems to be little we can do about it except, wherever possible, to "spread the load." If birds of a feather prefer to flock together, it is hard to keep them apart.

And have we the right to do so? This brings us to a point previously touched upon: the wishes of the immigrants themselves. As we have seen, some of the newcomers have no desire whatsoever to become assimilated, integrated, absorbed, or anything else. They want to make their pile and go home.

But many will stay, *malgré lui* in most cases; and what about them? Will they integrate? Those few who inter-marry will doubtless do so. At the other extreme are the Chinese, who keep themselves so much to themselves that their assimilation seems improbable. In between, the process seems likely to be slow.

Apart from the Chinese, the most anti-integrationist community is that of the Pakistanis, perhaps because they are Muslims and Islam's cloth has always incorporated a strong xenophobic strand. Hitherto an insufficient number of Muslim families have settled here to provide an answer to the question of whether the minds of children sent to English schools will be cast in a different mould. The few I came across or heard about seemed to have presented no special problems, except that girls had to skip physical training because their parents wouldn't allow them to undress and boys became the sole responsibility of their fathers after the age of six. Heads of nursery schools who wish to discuss a pupil with his parents normally deal with the mother; in the case of Pakistanis it is the father who calls.

6

It is the West Indians who most want to integrate. Amongst most communities of African origin a pale skin carries prestige. Conquering and ruling races pressing down from the north have generally been lighter in pigment than the true Negro, so pallor and prestige have forged a link. In the Caribbean it is smarter to be light-skinned than coal-black. Intermarriage with white people, the former masters, is in general smiled and seldom frowned upon.

It therefore appears that the group furthest away from us in physical appearance and pigmentation is the one we are most likely to assimilate. They share our language, faith, and culture, and as a community do not object.

Between Chinese and Pakistanis on the one hand and Caribbeans on the other lie a number of communities who really want a halfway house. Such are the Italians and Cypriots, Hungarians and Ukrainians, and above all, the Poles and the Jews, who came as exiles but need no longer be so if they wish; they have a country, now, to which most could repair. But very few will. They know that they are settlers and must settle, and yet they want—many Poles and Jews want with passion—to hold on to their identity, to preserve a nucleus at least of their tradition, to keep their language and not to be dissolved entirely in the all-devouring, all-pervading bloodstream of the host.

It can be done, and the Jews are here to prove it. Their

Diaspora lasted nearly two thousand years, and they have kept their identity. If the Jews can do it, so, perhaps, can Poles. There is the French Canadian example. India is a parcel of separate races, not a unity. In Ceylon there are Singhalese and Tamils; in Cyprus, Greeks and Turks; the instances are legion. Full integration is probably the exception, not the rule.

Should we object to this? Obviously not, if we believe in freedom; yet any large, undigested lump of foreigners lies heavy on the stomach of all nations at all times. It presses on some nerve that signals danger; unity is strength, separateness an invitation to conflict. (Look at Cyprus.) From this arises the threat to all minorities, of religion, of race, of ideology: Catholics or Protestants, Jews or Huguenots, Albigensians or Gnostics, Negroes or Armenians. Minorities have been persecuted either because they are small enough to bully, successful enough to pillage, or large enough to be feared. In Britain some are small enough, and some sufficiently successful, to qualify for persecution; instead they are being absorbed. None is, as yet, large enough to be feared, but this may need watching; and here we come back to the margin of safety, the threshold. Perhaps we are too impatient. You cannot take a bite like this and masticate it all at once. We think in years, and social change proceeds in generations.

So much comes back to the schools. Over them there hangs a question mark. We too easily assume that because children have no sense of race or colour when they are little racial coeducation will solve all. As we have seen, it doesn't. As children grow older, they draw apart. They absorb their parents' outlook and prejudices, and these harden like cysts in their growing minds. Their parents try to hold them. Outside their own group they make few close friends.

With adolescence comes sex rivalry; the young cocks spar-
ring, the male urge towards violence in this turbulent third
age of man; the transference of frustrations and your own
failures to the image of the alien, the eternal scapegoat. This
is a much more dangerous situation than that of the adult
immigrant arriving with his bundle of possessions, even if
you find he's taken the room next door with his uncouth
habits and queer-smelling stews. Here, at adolescence, where
the flash point is nearest, efforts to unite and blend the various communities have met with least success.

Can more be done? The trouble goes deep. What is needed
is a common cause to unite across dividing lines of community and race. This takes us back, once more, to another of
our starting points: that immigrants have created few new
problems, they have merely underscored those which already
perplex our society. In this case it is a lack of national purpose, of self-confidence, of belief; the malaise of crusaders
without a cross and youth without a cause; the end of an
imperial purpose that, right or wrong, sustained and mag-
nified us in the nineteenth century, collapsed in the twen-
tieth, and has left us in a vacuum now. This we can hardly
remedy as a by-product of absorbing immigrants.

Is there anything we *can* do? For a start, perhaps, sharpen
curiosity. Here are all these people from exotic backgrounds
in all corners of the world, full of strange lore and peculiar
ways. Most of us take no interest in them at all. We are idle;
language can be a barrier; on top of that, we are shy. But,
fundamentally, lazy. A television program on Barbados or
Nigeria, a feature on Sicilian politics or the Warsaw rising, is
less trouble and more informative than a halting conversation with the family next door. It's all predigested, and the

neighbour's English is poor. The human being tends nowadays to be a sort of filter, something that gets in the way.

Those who do take the trouble tend to do so from a sense
of duty rather than of exploration, taking pity on strangers in
a strange land. There's no need to pity them. They came of
their own free will—at least, all but the political refugees—in
their own self-interest, and most of them are doing well.
They don't want charity and don't need or deserve it.
They're not the lame ducks, but the energetic ones. "The
most enterprising of their race," it has been said, "live
amongst the least enterprising of ours."

Our idealists, progressives, and reformers, the activists of
our society, who march with banners to Aldermaston, squat
in Trafalgar Square, sign petitions and letters to *The Times,*
and fill the office of the voice of conscience from which Chris-
tianity, by and large, has been evicted—these individuals
leave us in no doubt of the wickedness of apartheid in South
Africa, of segregation in America, of the Portuguese in Africa
who won't gracefully bow themselves out. They condemn
with equal spirit, in their native land, colour-conscious landladies, protesting parents, local officials who shy away from
turbans, any sign of colour prejudice wherever it may rear its
head. Fair enough. But I sometimes wonder how many of the
paraders, demonstrators, petitioners, and inveighers have
ever asked a Jamaican bus conductor, a Pakistani factory
hand, an Indian shopkeeper, a Cypriot cafe owner, a Polish
toolmaker, a Nigerian nurse, or a Lithuanian wardmaid
home to tea.

Bibliography

A Minority in Britain. Maurice Freedman. Valentine & Mitchell, 1955.

Anglo-Egyptian Resettlement Board. Reports 1957–60.

"An Anglo-Jewish Community: Leeds." Ernest Krausz. *Jewish Journal of Sociology,* Vol. IV, No. 1.

Britain in the Sixties: Housing. Stanley Alderson. Penguin Special, 1962.

Coloured Immigrants in Britain. Survey by Institute of Race Relations, 1960.

Coloured Immigrants in Leeds. Eric Butterworth. Institute of Adult Education & Extra-Mural Studies, University of Leeds, 1963.

Commonwealth Immigrants Act, 1962. Statistics, 1962–63. Her Majesty's Stationery Office Cmd. 2151, October 1963.

Dark Strangers. Sheila Patterson. Tavistock Press, 1963.

"The Distribution of Immigrant Groups in London." R. B. Davison. *Race,* October 1963.

Ethnic Prejudice and Choice of Friends Among English and non-English Adolescents. T. Kawwa. Institute of Education, University of London.

Field Marshal Lord Ligonier: A Story of the British Army, 1702–1770. Rex Whitworth. Oxford University Press, 1958.

Housing. Ministry of Housing & Local Government. Cmd. 2050, May 1963.

The Immigrant in Bradford. Report of Bradford Social Workers' Conference, 1960.

"Immigrant Groups in London." R. B. Davison. *Race,* April 1961. Institute of Race Relations.

"Immigration." *Economist Intelligence Unit,* 1961.

Indian Immigrants in Britain. Rashmi Desai. Oxford University Press for Institute of Race Relations, 1963.

"Indian University Students in Britain." Political and Economic Planning, Vol. XXVII, No. 456, November 1961.

Institute of Education, University of Nottingham. Report of Conference on Immigrants, 1962.

Inter-marriage and Jewish Life: A Symposium. Ed. Werner J. Cahman. Herxl Press, New York, 1963. Paper by L. Rosenberg.

The Irish in Britain. John A. Jackson. Routledge & Kegan Paul, 1963.

Leeds Jewry: Its History and Social Structure. Ernest Krausz. The Jewish Historical Society in England, 1964.

Leeds Tercentenary of the Resettlement of the Jews. Leeds Jewish Representative Council, November 1956.

Negroes in Britain. K. L. Little. Kegan Paul, 1948.

Newcomers. Ruth Glass. Centre for Urban Studies.

"Occupation and Social Advancement in Anglo-Jewry." Ernest Krausz. *Jewish Journal of Sociology,* Vol. IV, No. 1.

Overseas Migration Board. Statistics for 1962. Commonwealth Relations Office. Cmd. 2217, 1963.

Overseas Students in Britain. The British Council, London, 1962.

The Pakistanis in London. Hamza Alavi. British Overseas Socialist Fellowship.

Parliamentary Debates (Hansard). House of Commons, November 22, 1957. Debate on Housing, London (immigrants).

"A Policy for Housing." *Economist Intelligence Unit.* Michael Gardner, 1963.

"The Polish Exile Community in Britain." Sheila Patterson. *The Polish Review,* Vol. VI, No. 3, 1961. (U.S.A.)

Polish Immigrants in Britain. Jerzy Zubrzycki. The Hague, 1956.

Refugees in Britain: Hungarians and Anglo-Egyptians. Political and Economic Planning, Vol. XXIV, No. 419, 1958.

They Came As Strangers. Francesca Wilson. Hamish Hamilton, 1959.

West Indian Migrants. R. B. Davison. Oxford University Press, 1962.

West Indian Migrants and the London Churches. Rev. Clifford Hill. Oxford University Press for Institute of Race Relations, 1963.

APPENDIX A

Estimated Total Net Immigration into U.K., 1946–62

Country	Number	Percentage of total
Australia	80,850	7.5
Canada	18,000	1.7
Ceylon	6,300	0.6
Cyprus	33,400	3.1
East Africa	8,900	0.8
Federation Rhodesia and Nyasaland	5,600	0.5
India and Pakistan	150,900	14.0
Malaya	8,100	0.7
Malta	16,400	1.5
New Zealand	23,400	2.2
West Africa	20,400	1.9
West Indies	263,700	24.4
Other Commonwealth Countries	23,300	2.1
Total Commonwealth	659,250	61.0
Irish	421,850	39.0
TOTAL	1,081,100	100.0

APPENDIX B

Estimated Net Inward Movement of Commonwealth Migrants

Country of Origin	1955	1956	1957	1958	1959	1960	1961	First six months of 1962	July, 1962– June 30, 1963
Cyprus	27,550	29,800	23,000	15,000	16,400	49,650	66,300	31,800	26,040
East Africa	5,800	5,600	6,600	6,200	2,950	5,900	23,750	19,050	19,906
Hong Kong	1,850	2,050	5,200	4,700	850	2,500	25,100	25,080	15,748
India	3,450	2,750	1,450	2,700	400	3,200	6,850	3,150	6,798
Pakistan	700	700	650	400	150	250	2,650	1,980	10,931
West Africa	1,500	2,000	2,200	950	750	−500	5,450	6,630	14,040
West Indies	300	550	900	200	450	500	2,150	2,160	4,632
Others	1,550	3,400	2,400	−300	−350	−3,800	4,150	5,050	17,675
Total	42,700	46,850	42,400	29,850	21,600	57,700	136,400	94,900	115,770

APPENDIX C

Immigration from the Commonwealth

TABLE I

JANUARY 1, 1963–DECEMBER 31, 1963

Territory	Holders of Ministry of Labour vouchers (1)	Students (2)	Dependents accommodated or coming to join the head of the household, and other persons coming for settlement (3)	Others (mainly visitors and "returning visitors") (4)	Admitted (Total of columns 1-4) (5)	Embarked (6)	Net Balance (7)
India	8,366	2,085	7,117	24,541	42,109	24,611	+17,498
Pakistan	13,526	1,158	3,545	11,344	29,573	13,237	+16,336
West Indies*	2,077	1,984	9,041	13,984	27,086	19,158	+ 7,928
All other overseas Commonwealth territories	6,156	13,257	9,978	287,578	266,969	242,731	+24,238
Totals	30,125	18,484	29,681	287,447	365,737	299,737	+66,000

* Jamaica, Trinidad and Tobago, Barbados, Leeward and Windward islands, and British Guiana.

NOTES:

1. There is no control on traffic between Ireland and Britain.

2. The above figures include persons enjoying diplomatic immunity, who are recorded for statistical purposes although exempt from control under Section 17 of the act.

185

TABLE II

Estimated net inward movement from	1959	1960	1961	1962 (January–June only)
India	2,950	5,900	23,750	19,050
Pakistan	850	2,500	25,100	25,080
West Indies*	16,400	49,650	66,300	31,800
Other Territories†	1,400	−350	21,250	18,970

A minus sign denotes a net *outward* movement.

* Includes, with the former Federation of the West Indies, British Guiana and British Honduras.

† Excluding Canada, Australia, New Zealand, and the Federation of Rhodesia and Nyasaland, for which no estimates are available.

INDEX